THE UTOPIA PLAYBOOK

Secrets to an ideal world –
from the most inspiring countries

AYESHA S. RATNAYAKE

THE UTOPIA PLAYBOOK

Copyright © 2023 by Ayesha Ratnayake

For permission requests, write to the publisher at hi@cheatsheets.life.

For my mother and father,
who made me believe everything is possible.

"You may say I'm a dreamer, but I'm not the only one."
John Lennon

CONTENTS

INTRODUCTION

Utopia /juːˈtəʊpɪə/ (noun):

An imagined place or state of things in which everything is perfect.

I dream of living in Utopia. A world where everybody leads happy, long and healthy lives. Where everyone is free to achieve their fullest potential, bolstered by a society free from discrimination and an education system that inspires and empowers. A world where we can all breathe clean air and take pride in the fact that we aren't destroying our home planet or harming its creatures. A world where the environment is green, beautiful and accommodating of our needs. A world free from poverty, bursting with abundance and generosity, with systems of governance that we can trust.

And I believe such a world is possible. Because I've seen it. I've caught glimpses of it in the classrooms of Finland and the forests of Bhutan. I've spotted it in the busy corridors of Swiss hospitals and the cosy side streets of Colombia. Yes, I've even shadowed it in parliaments, from Denmark to Rwanda to New Zealand.

Trust me. Utopia is out there.

This book will be your guide on a tour of the world's many mini utopias. Read on to discover which country has a Minister for Loneliness and where 40% of commutes are made by bicycle. Learn how one nation used a chessboard approach to design a garden city and what the world's lowest energy-per-kilometre rail system looks like. Find out why one country has led the world in organ donation for three decades and how 'sharing cities' are transforming communities. And uncover hundreds more insights to envision – and build – an ideal world.

We'll explore the places of peak happiness, health, equality and abundance – and along the way, we'll learn how these places came to be so special. And more importantly, how we might be able to make any place a little bit more utopian.

The Utopia Playbook is for everyday citizens who dream of a better world. It is for current and future educators, activists, economists, policymakers, politicians and pressure groups. Because whether you are suffering in a failed country or curious about how much better things could be, you deserve to live in Utopia. And through your actions – whether by smart voting, lobbying for change, becoming an entrepreneur, or running for office – you can create a utopia right where you are.

I'll show you where to look for inspiration.

1
Happiness

A recipe for contentment

"Contentment consists not in adding more fuel,
but in taking away some fire."
Thomas Fuller, British author

It goes without saying that the inhabitants of Utopia would be happy and content. But what does that even mean? Is it possible to measure happiness?

The creators of the World Happiness Report seem to think so. According to Jeff Sachs, Columbia University professor and co-creator of the World Happiness Report, when researchers talk about "happiness," what they really mean is "satisfaction with the way one's life is going". The measure asks: "Please imagine a ladder, with steps numbered from 0 at the bottom to 10 at the top. The top of the ladder represents the best possible life for you and the bottom of the ladder represents the worst possible life for you. On which step of the ladder would you say you personally feel you stand at this time?

*"It's not primarily a measure of whether one
laughed or smiled yesterday, but how one
feels about the course of one's life."*
Jeff Sachs, co-creator of the World Happiness Report

So, based on this measure, which country is the happiest? For over five years in a row (as at 2023), **Finland** has been named the happiest country in the world. On a scale of 1 to 10, Finnish citizens evaluate their lives at an average of 7.804. After Finland, **Denmark** comes in at second place, followed by **Iceland**, **Israel**, and the **Netherlands**.

But why is a nation from the northern corner of the world, with a cold climate and six months of winter and darkness, the happiest in the world? And what could it be that makes people in happy countries so happy? Let's take a look.

MEETING CITIZENS' BASIC NEEDS

Ensuring a decent quality of life

Is being rich the reason citizens of these countries are so satisfied with their lives? According to research, wealth does have a role to play. But perhaps, not to the extent you might expect. While the Nordic countries do report high GDP per capita, countries with much higher GDP per capita are not nearly as happy. For example, the average household disposable income in the United States (which ranks 15th on the 2023 World Happiness Index) is about USD 45,000, while in top-ranking **Finland** and **Denmark**, it's around USD 30,000.

It turns out that while *not* having money causes unhappiness, once you are able to meet a decent standard of living, an even higher income doesn't generate as much happiness.

*"The Gross National Product measures everything
except that which makes life worthwhile."*
Robert Kennedy, former United States Attorney General

While life expectancy tends to increase, up to a per capita GDP of about USD 5,000 a year, once there's enough to meet basic living standards, GDP becomes less important. Social issues can continue despite high GDP – including child mortality, obesity, drug and alcohol abuse, depression, teen pregnancies, low literacy, crime, murder, low life expectancy, and social immobility. Indeed, the United States and Portugal rank side by side for social issues although the USA has more than double Portugal's GDP per capita!

So, if getting as rich as possible isn't the key to a country's happiness, what's going on?

It turns out that once citizens have enough to eat, the factor that is a far more effective predictor of citizen welfare is... equality.

As it happens, the Nordic countries, which rank at the pinnacle for global happiness, also tend to have cultures designed around the belief in human equality. These countries strive to ensure that citizens at the bottom of the socioeconomic ladder are able to lead lives of dignity and meet their basic needs. For example, **Denmark**'s rate of child poverty is about a quarter of that of the United States. And another leader in happiness, **Iceland**, has the region's lowest poverty rate (9%). **Finland** too has very little poverty and there's no need for anyone to be homeless. Finnish citizens enjoy free healthcare and a free education system that is world-renowned and has been deemed one of the fairest in Europe.

Over in **Costa Rica**, the Latin American leader for happiness, citizens enjoy more happiness per GDP dollar than just about any other place.

Some of the reasons include universal healthcare and education. Most villages have free primary care clinics and, since 1869, primary school has been free and compulsory for every child.

Beyond this, in happy countries, those at the top of the socioeconomic ladder seem to avoid showing off their wealth. The richest people in **Finland** might choose to drive an old Volvo or (at most) a Mercedes, rather than splurging on a Lamborghini. This attitude of modesty prevails in **Denmark** too. It is sometimes referred to as the 'Law of Jante' based on the code of conduct in a work of fiction by a Danish-Norwegian author which demands 'You are not to believe you are more valuable than anyone else'.

> *"In Denmark, few have too much,*
> *and even fewer have too little."*
> *Nikolai Frederik Severin Grundtvig,*
> *1820 Danish thinker and priest*

Such a culture of humility supports social equality and community spirit – two factors that the World Happiness Report states are closely linked to happiness.

The following chart shows how the level of income inequality in the Nordic countries compares with that of less happy nations. As you can see, the happier Nordic countries are also significantly more equal.

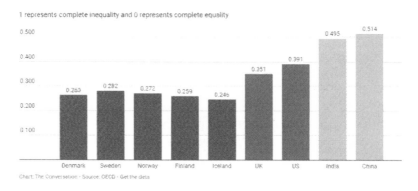

1 represents complete inequality and 0 represents complete equality

Chart: The Conversation · Source: OECD · Get the data

Relative levels of income inequality; Source: The Conversation, OECD

But isn't taking care of everyone expensive?

In Nordic countries, high living standards across the socioeconomic spectrum are achieved through a high rate of taxation. Indeed, Danish citizens pay some of the highest income taxes in the world, starting at 41%, with the richest individuals paying 56% of their income in tax. Besides paying taxes on their income, people in **Denmark** also pay a 25% value-added tax on most items. This rate can go much higher, with new cars requiring a tax payment of up to 150%.

But wait, doesn't paying high taxes reduce happiness?

It turns out that high taxes aren't a problem when it means great living standards. Most Danish citizens are glad to pay taxes as the benefits are plainly visible. They see it as an investment in quality of life.

These are just some of the ways Danes reap the returns of high taxes:

- Attending university tuition-free
- Receiving a grant to help manage expenses when studying
- Being able to access free healthcare
- Enjoying subsidised childcare

- Receiving pensions after retirement
- Having care helpers visit their home to take care of them when they are elderly

Danish citizens appreciate that if everyone contributes, a social safety net can be provided to support the very old, the very young, and the sick. They believe in supporting the common good and accepting the responsibility to work if able. Indeed, none of Denmark's nine major political parties seriously support changing Denmark's system of taxation and social welfare provision.

Around the world, institutions offering universal social welfare tend to persist over time, even if the government subsequently changes. This can be seen in the Nordic countries, as well as in the United Kingdom (where no party has eliminated the National Health Service), Canada (where all governments have retained the single-payer healthcare system) and the United States (where Social Security has never been dismantled).

Absorbing risks to empower citizens

The Nordic countries boast high rates of employment, and this itself contributes to happiness. The World Happiness Report found that being unable to work during the COVID-19 pandemic reduced wellbeing, with unemployment connected to a 12% drop in life satisfaction.

But the Nordic countries also recognise that life doesn't always follow a neat trajectory and support citizens who need to make a change. In **Denmark**, the social safety net that comes from high taxes also supports people who lose their jobs for up to two years while they look for new jobs, with a system in place to make sure they are actively looking for work. For example, a Danish citizen Christina received about USD 2000 a month from the Danish government while she was unemployed. This safety net empowers people with the freedom to pursue work that will make them feel fulfilled and happy, instead of clinging to a miserable job simply to make ends meet.

"Danes feel empowered to change things in their lives. What is special about Danish society is that it allows people to choose the kind of life they want to live."
Christian Bjørnskov, Professor of Economics,
Aarhus University

Efforts are made to support individuals experiencing all types of difficulty. In fact, the Danish municipality of Aarhus has created an online portal (socialkompasset.dk) collating the free services available from the municipality and volunteer organisations to support individuals in need, including abuse victims, individuals struggling with addiction, refugees, immigrants and others. The portal, now being transformed into a nationwide project, provides access to a wide range of services, from free legal support to homework assistance.

Other countries are also taking measures to support citizens in getting back on their feet. In 2022, the **French** government began covering the cost of therapy sessions for youth and adults with mental health concerns. The government covers the cost of an initial consultation at about USD 40 and seven additional sessions of around USD 30, with the ability to renew.

APPROACHING HAPPINESS SIDEWAYS

Prioritising contentment

And yet, the citizens of the happiest countries are not necessarily bubbly and jubilant. Instead, they seem to be living examples of John Stuart Mill's quote "Happiness should be approached sideways, like a crab".

Denmark's happiness is "not happiness, it is contentment. The Danes take their time doing things. They're not stressed," states a Danish citizen, Crispin Avon of Copenhagen. "Contrary to popular belief, you don't see Danes smiling or getting overexcited very often. Happiness here is more to do with the practicalities of living," affirms Andy Keefe of Horsens, Denmark.

In fact, the Danes have two words for happiness – "lykke" which suggests elusiveness, and "glad" which expresses regular contentment. The Danish language embraces the idea that moments of peak glee are elusive, while regular satisfaction with life is normal. This sets realistic expectations for what a good life looks like.

Helsinki Times reports that, compared to much of the Western world, **Finland** is more laidback, warm, cooperative and at peace with itself. Finnish citizens feel comfortable and avoid stressing about the outside world, giving them the resilience to manage life's stressors.

Going one step further, The New York Times reports that Finns embrace depictions of themselves as melancholic and reserved. Indeed, a popular Finnish joke goes "An introverted Finn looks at his shoes when talking to you; an extroverted Finn looks at your shoes". People in Finland tend to have realistic expectations for their lives and to be content to be what they are. Sari Poyhonen, a linguistics professor at the University of Jyvaskyla, describes how when something in life does exceed expectations, Finns will often act with humility, preferring a self-deprecating joke over bragging.

"Finns are pros at keeping their happiness a secret."
Sari Poyhonen, Linguistics Professor, University of Jyvaskyla

Valuing relaxation and downtime

Relaxation is a priority in countries that rank at the top of the World Happiness Index. **Danes** even have a word for cosy relaxation: "hygge" (pronounced 'hoo-guh'). The concept roughly translates to taking a break from the daily hubbub to enjoy life's simple pleasures, and it can be enjoyed either with family and friends or alone. The experience of "hygge" can range from cosy game nights with loved ones and fireside chats over hot drinks to nature walks over long winter months or settling down with a good book or TV show.

In **Finland**, saunas are the name of the game. These steamy environments stimulate muscle relaxation and prompt the release of endorphins. They are also a critical part of the Finnish culture – in 2018, there were around 2.3 million saunas in Finland for a population of 5.5 million! Many workplaces offer both sauna and gym facilities. This isn't pure indulgence – according to Matleena Livson from the Finnish Sports Confederation, research supports that investing in employee wellbeing can generate a 6X return.

Another way in which the Nordic countries prioritise downtime is by valuing vacations. European Union labour laws guarantee workers a minimum of four weeks of paid annual vacation, apart from holidays, sick days and parental leave. In Finland, after working with a company for one year, employees are typically entitled to four weeks of vacation in the summer and one week of vacation in the winter.

Employees in happy countries tend to spend less time at work. While the average OECD country sees 10% of its employees working long hours (50 or more hours a week), in **Denmark**, that percentage drops to just 1%. Compared with employees in the United States, the typical Danish worker enjoys about 150 additional hours of annual leisure time. According to Tom Gibson of Copenhagen, an everyday reflection of Denmark's happiness is that streets are crowded with bikes at 8:30 am instead of being crowded with cars at 7:30 am, and grocery stores are crowded at 5:00 pm instead of 6:30 pm. **Iceland**, found in a study to be the least stressed European nation, also has the shortest commutes (only 15 minutes on average).

Other countries are also taking steps to promote a relaxed workforce. In the **United Kingdom**, a law entitles any employee to request flexible working hours or the chance to work from home – and employers can be taken to an employment tribunal if they refuse a request without good reason.

Meanwhile, in **Portugal**, it is now illegal for bosses to contact employees after working hours – with penalties if they do. The country has also joined nations like **Spain**, **Scotland**, **Japan** and **Belgium** in experimenting with a four-day workweek. But it is **Iceland** that is the pioneer in this space. A trial conducted from 2015 to 2019 was a major success, dramatically boosting employee wellbeing and reducing stress and burnout while retaining or improving productivity. As a result, nearly 90% of Icelandic workers now enjoy reduced working hours.

Embracing nature and exercise

Leisure time in happy countries is often spent exercising. **Finns** will gladly brave rain, snow or cold wind for the chance to go out jogging or cycling. Warmer summer weather means everything from cycling and hiking to kayaking, camping, and more.

"One of the first conditions of happiness is that the link between man and nature shall not be broken."
Leo Tolstoy, Russian writer

Being surrounded by nature and getting out into it has long been known to boost happiness, and this seems to be the case for the Finns. Having over 73% of its land covered in greenery, Finland boasts impressive natural beauty, wildlife, low pollution levels and clean air. With pristine forests and crystal-clear lakes, there is much to see and do outdoors. In fact, the Finnish city of Lahti has even installed "forest workstations" to encourage its residents to work remotely from relaxing natural sites. These minimalistic wooden workstations blend into the surroundings while including space for laptops, bags and mobile phones.

FOSTERING A SENSE OF COMMUNITY

Cherishing social connection

Social ties have a key role to play in building happiness, so it's no wonder that citizens of happy countries seem to enjoy significant social connections. The majority of **Costa Ricans** report being not just satisfied but thriving in their social relationships. Family and religion play a central part in Costa Rican culture, promoting regular social interaction. This helps place Costa Rica among the countries where people experience the most positive emotions day-to-day.

Meanwhile, in **Denmark**, over 90% of people are part of a club or association and more than 40% volunteer in civic groups. Such regular opportunities for community engagement provide Danes with a solid sense of connection.

Normalising trust

Another vital factor among happy countries is trust, and the Nordic countries score top marks in this domain as well. In fact, people in Scandinavia even feel comfortable leaving babies in strollers outside coffee shops while they run errands. Each morning in **Finland**, children as young as seven can be seen walking alone to school in complete security. This is true in **Switzerland** too, also in the top 10 of the Happiness Index. In **Denmark**, it isn't unusual for eight or nine-year-olds to navigate public transport by themselves. Meanwhile, 95% of Danes believe they have someone they can depend on in a time of need. In personal relationships, business and government, Danes default towards trusting one another.

How safe people feel is a key measure of happiness in the World Happiness Report. Low crime levels mean that **Finland** performs well in this area. Indeed, when basic services are available for everyone, there is much less poverty and feelings of injustice. This, in turn, reduces crime.

Cultivating honesty and generosity

Unsurprisingly, countries with low levels of corruption, where the government is seen to be credible and honest, tend to rank higher for happiness.

According to Transparency International, **Finland**, **Denmark**, **Norway** and **Sweden** are among the six least corrupt countries as at 2021. As a result, their citizens enjoy feelings of trust and security. Jeffrey Sachs, co-editor of the World Happiness Report, has said that apart from social support, the top contributors to national happiness are honesty in government and citizen generosity. To a great extent, these countries have both.

> *"Danish happiness is closely tied to their notion of 'tryghed', the snuggled, tucked-in feeling that begins with a mother's love and extends to the relationship Danes have with their government. The system doesn't so much ensure happiness as it keeps people from doing what will make them unhappy."*
> *Jonathan Schwartz, Copenhagen-based*
> *American anthropologist*

The Nordic countries are known to be generous towards the rest of the world. For 40 years, **Denmark** has been one of only five countries worldwide (three of which are Nordic countries) to meet the United Nations' target of allocating 0.7% of Gross National Income (GNI) towards development assistance. This benefits its citizens too – the World Happiness Report stresses that people are happier when they feel they live in a generous society.

DESIGNING HAPPINESS BY POLICY

In contrast to the pictures of happiness shown in the media, the Nordic countries seem to have greater wisdom about what creates true happiness. They understand that luxury lifestyles don't bring contentment, but personal freedoms and access to basic living standards do. They don't seek lavish displays of wealth, but relaxation, exercise and time in nature. They understand that working long hours without balance is neither desirable nor productive. And all this wisdom reaps vast rewards in life satisfaction.

Of course, we need to remember that these top-ranking countries for happiness are quite homogeneous when it comes to ethnicity and religion. They are also small countries – Denmark has fewer than 6 million citizens. And the picture isn't entirely rosy. In fact, Denmark used to see high suicide rates, though they have now dropped to a quarter of what they used to be. It seems that living in a country where most other people are satisfied with their lives can make it extra difficult to be the unhappy outlier.

Despite these caveats, the Nordic countries point the way to a model of happiness that prioritises looking after citizens across the socioeconomic strata, protecting people from insecurity, and encouraging the pursuit of contented, wholesome, generous living over high-stress, fast-paced and luxurious lifestyles.

Zooming out of the Nordic region, several countries have introduced initiatives to promote happiness and wellbeing among citizens. Let's explore some of these efforts.

Bhutan's Gross National Happiness Index

"Gross National Happiness is more important
than Gross Domestic Product."
King Jigme Singye Wangchuck, fourth king of Bhutan

Since 1972, when King Jigme Singye Wangchuck made this now-famous declaration, the idea of Gross National Happiness has generated intrigue worldwide. The Gross National Happiness Index seeks to reflect the general wellbeing of the **Bhutanese** population and includes socio-economic factors such as living standards, health and education, as well as aspects of culture and psychological wellbeing.

The Index measures every citizen's wellbeing status across 33 indicators and classifies them as unhappy, narrowly happy, extensively happy, or deeply happy. This analysis considers the areas where people already demonstrate happiness and is used as a starting point to evaluate how policies can be used to boost happiness and sufficiency among those groups who rate as unhappy or narrowly happy. Like countries which boast the happiest citizens, Bhutan provides free healthcare facilities and education (up to high school).

UAE's Minister for Happiness and Wellbeing

In 2016, the **United Arab Emirates** announced a Minister of State for Happiness and Wellbeing, Ohood bint Khalfan Al Roumi. Al Roumi's programme was based on three themes: happiness and positivity in government work, happiness and positivity in lifestyle, and the measurement of happiness and positivity. Accordingly, she engaged in initiatives such as these:

- Conducting a national happiness survey and an employee happiness survey
- Introducing online "happiness meters" in city offices where people could record their satisfaction by clicking on emojis
- Sending 60 "Chief Happiness and Positivity Officers" to Oxford University, UC Berkeley, etc. to be trained on how to create a more positive workforce
- Organising a global dialogue on happiness, bringing together international academics, scientists, government leaders and organisations to discuss the advancement of human happiness
- Unveiling a "Happiness Patrol" where police replace handing out traffic tickets with rewarding law-abiding motorists with gift vouchers and mobile phone credit

Ecuador's State Secretary of "Buen Vivir"

In 2013, **Ecuador** introduced a state secretary of "buen vivir" – a phrase that roughly translates to "good living" or "wellbeing." Among the proposed policies were meditation lessons for schoolchildren and labelling foods based on nutritional value. However, unlike the failed efforts of nearby Venezuela which created a Vice Ministry of Supreme Social Happiness, Ecuador did see a nominal boost in happiness over the following five years, according to the World Happiness Index.

United Kingdom's Minister for Loneliness

In 2018, the **United Kingdom** introduced a Minister for Loneliness and published a government loneliness strategy. The Office of National Statistics was tasked with measuring loneliness and set up a fund of around USD 14 million to support 126 projects to transform the lives of thousands of lonely people across England. It also introduced a #LetsTalkLoneliness awareness campaign and podcast, and a Loneliness Advice chatbot service on WhatsApp.

2
Health

*"Healthy citizens are
the greatest asset any country can have."
Winston Churchill, former prime minister
of the United Kingdom*

No Utopia is complete without a fountain of youth to ensure longevity and lifelong good health. As of 2020, the average person can expect to live to 73 years. However, there are a handful of countries where the average citizen can expect to live a decade beyond that number.

Wealthy Asian countries top the charts for life expectancy, beginning with **Hong Kong** and **Japan** where, as at 2020, the average citizen can expect to live to 85 years. **Singapore** (average lifespan of 84 years) and the Republic of **Korea** (average lifespan of 83 years) are close behind.

Iceland, **Switzerland** and **Norway** are all leaders in Europe, while **Australia** and **Israel** also provide international benchmarks. All these countries boast an average lifespan of 83 years. In case you're wondering, citizens of the happy nations of **Finland** and **Denmark** can expect to live to 82 years on average. Indeed, life expectancy has a proven role in happiness – it's hard to be happy when you aren't healthy.

When it comes to lifespan, the island of Okinawa in **Japan** is especially remarkable, with residents enjoying a 40% greater chance of seeing their 100th birthday than other Japanese people. In **Italy**, where the average life expectancy is 82 years, the island of Sardinia also boasts a large concentration of centenarians, including an equal ratio of male and female centenarians.

What secrets do these nations hold for a long life? Let's take a peek into what it takes to foster a healthy citizenry.

PROVIDING A GREAT START IN LIFE

When discussing health, it's a good idea to begin at the beginning. In the book 'Upstream: How to Solve Problems Before They Happen', Dan Heath describes how some countries invest in proactive, upstream solutions more than reactive, downstream ones. For example, an individual can be stopped from performing a robbery by seeing an alarm system – a downstream solution – or by being assisted towards a better path during her youth – an upstream solution.

Developed countries spend 2 dollars upstream for every dollar spent downstream. **Norway** goes further, spending 2.50 dollars upstream for every dollar spent downstream. As an example, the nation takes early childhood care very seriously. Prenatal and postnatal care in Norway is free, and the country offers lots of paid maternity and paternity leave. Talk about beginning at the beginning!

The other Nordic countries also boast impressive track records of maternal and child care. For example, mothers in **Denmark** can expect

18 weeks of fully paid maternity leave, and everyone can take advantage of subsidised child care.

Finland – which has achieved one of the world's lowest infant mortality rates – has a unique tradition to guarantee all children an equally good start in life, no matter what background they're from. For 75 years, every Finnish expectant mother has been entitled to receive a gift box from the government containing loads of items for their newborn. They can choose between the box or a cash grant of approximately USD 170. 95% choose the box as it's far more valuable.

Here's a peek at what's inside:

- Mattress, mattress cover, blanket, undersheet, duvet cover, sleeping bag/quilt
- Bodysuits, romper suits and leggings
- Cloth nappy set, nappy cream and muslin squares
- Hooded bath towel, bath thermometer, washcloth
- Nail scissors, hairbrush, toothbrush
- Picture book and teething toy
- Snowsuit, knitted hat, socks, balaclava (winter face mask), insulated mittens and booties
- Light hooded suit and knitted overalls

Plus, the box itself can be used as a crib! Babies from all socioeconomic settings have their first naps within the box, helping parents implement research that it is healthier for babies to sleep outside their parents' beds. The box also now intentionally excludes baby bottles and dummies to encourage breastfeeding.

While the scheme was initially only offered to low-income families, from 1949, it was made available to all pregnant women. Expectant mothers must also visit a doctor or municipal clinic before their fourth month of pregnancy to claim the box. This helps ensure that mothers-to-be get appropriate medical care and guidance while providing them with the necessary items to care for their newborns. The concept has been a runaway success. In 2016, Finland had the world's lowest rate of child mortality, while in 2015, it had the lowest rate of maternal mortality.

Finland continues to prioritise child health as kids enter school, with free school meals provided to all children. The country has even initiated a school garden programme. In the spring, students grow indoor plants, prepare the soil, and plant and sow seeds. In autumn, they collect the yield and prepare the soil for winter. Studies affirm that if children grow their own food, they are also more likely to eat it. In **India** too, the country with the largest undernourished population, all schools are now required to have 'nutrition gardens' where children can learn how to grow their own food, even in crowded urban environments. Seeds and saplings, organic manure, training and technical help are provided by appointed agencies.

Ezekiel Emanuel, author of 'Which Country Has the World's Best Healthcare?' and co-director of the University of Pennsylvania's Health Transformation Institute, when asked about healthcare reform in the United States, recommended early childhood interventions should be made in the US as well: "The highest return investment that the United States can make is in early childhood interventions, especially for children born into poverty, which is now 40 to 50% of the American birth cohort. (...) Those early childhood interventions, as Jim Heckman at the University of Chicago has shown, returned $7 to $15 per kid. I would also make child care veritably free. That experiment has been tried in Montreal. It actually pays for itself very quickly. That is a huge second investment I would make. A third investment I would make is to make pre-K (a voluntary classroom-based preschool programme for children below the age of five in the United States) universal, required, and free."

"So you can see, all of my investments are investing in kids."
Ezekiel Emanuel, author of 'Which Country Has
the World's Best Healthcare?'

GUARANTEEING AFFORDABLE HEALTHCARE

Today, a woman in **Japan** can expect to live to 88 and a man to 82. But this hasn't always been the case. In fact, it represents a 30-year increase in lifespan since 1947. How did Japan achieve this remarkable boost in outcomes?

When the Japanese economy saw rapid growth in the 1950s and 1960s, the government began to invest heavily in public health, introducing universal health insurance, free tuberculosis treatment, childhood vaccinations and effective treatment of infections. As at 2014, 84% of healthcare costs are covered by public spending. The country continues to prioritise affordable healthcare to date and, during the COVID-19 pandemic, free school lunches were provided to families in need.

In **Hong Kong,** which tops the world for life expectancy, universal healthcare is available for hospital treatment. "When you're sick, really sick and need to be hospitalised, it's free at the point of care, paid for by taxation," says Dr Gabriel Leung, Dean of the Faculty of Medicine at Hong Kong University. "Nobody would be denied adequate medical care due to lack of means," affirms Dr John Beard, Director of the Department of Ageing and Life Course at the World Health Organisation.

"It's important that access is for everybody, not just the rich. That's
when the average life expectancy will increase."
Dr John Beard, Director of the Department of Ageing and Life
Course, World Health Organisation

Singapore has a unique approach. Employees are required to divert about 37% of their salaries towards mandatory savings accounts. These may be used for healthcare, housing, education, insurance or investment expenses, with employers contributing to a portion of the amount. Cheap or free healthcare is provided in government-run hospital wards while more deluxe care is also available in private rooms for those willing to pay more. The government uses bulk purchasing power to spend less on drugs. It also regulates the number of medical students and physicians in the country and has a say in how much they can earn. The system is unorthodox but works. In 2017, the country with the lowest number of 'lost' years due to poor health (or Disability Adjusted Life Years) was Singapore. Yet, remarkably, the health system costs only 4.9% of the GDP.

Switzerland takes a different approach to ensuring universally accessible healthcare. It has a system called Santésuisse, requiring everyone to buy insurance. Private insurance companies offer insurance plans on a non-profit basis. These plans are community rated and must be provided to any eligible applicant regardless of their health status. Depending on income, subsidies are provided to offset insurance premium costs. Almost 30% of people take advantage of these. Insurers can also offer for-profit coverage for additional services and more choice in hospitals. This system seems to work well for the Swiss, who perform well on longevity, infant mortality, and physical and mental health, and even have among the shortest hospital waiting times.

Also among the countries with the longest life expectancy, **Australia** provides free inpatient care in public hospitals, as well as free access to most medical services and prescription drugs. Citizens may also use private hospitals and private health insurance if they wish.

Norway too has a strong subsidised system that supports the poor and offers low drug prices, with 85% of healthcare costs covered by public spending as at 2019. Here, private spending on healthcare makes up less than USD 100 per person. And thanks to free vaccinations for Norwegian children, over 96% of kids are vaccinated against key ailments. Doctors play a big part in encouraging healthy living and can even prescribe physical activity as a treatment.

Another factor that seems to be correlated with longer lifespans is a low level of income inequality. For example, a flatter social gradient is credited as playing a part in **Italy**'s high life expectancy, which stands out even while the country lags behind other European nations in wealth and healthcare spending. And a smaller gap between the haves and have-nots has been suggested to contribute to **Australians**' long lifespans too. Relative equality in the 1970s is reputed to have played a role in **Japan**'s high life expectancy rates as well.

Affordable healthcare access matters. In high-income countries, households typically don't need to spend a lot out-of-pocket for healthcare. This is because high-income countries tend to rely on public spending to cover healthcare costs.

The United States is perhaps the only developed nation without universal healthcare. Despite being one of the richest countries and spending more on healthcare as a share of the economy (nearly double the average OECD country), the United States has the lowest life expectancy (77 years in 2020) out of the 11 OECD nations. This is more than two years fewer than the OECD average and five years fewer than Switzerland. At over USD 4,000 per person, private spending is more than five times that spent by the second highest spending nation, Canada. There's also a large administrative cost associated with the many different insurance programmes on offer, which adds to both cost and complexity.

OPTIMISING LIFESTYLES

Encouraging healthy diets

The way a nation's citizens eat and live naturally influences their lifespan. According to Dr Timothy Kwok, professor of geriatric medicine at the Chinese University of **Hong Kong**, citizens in this region enjoy the longest lifespans in part due to access to good food. Diets typically comprise fruit and vegetables, fresh fish, rice, nut oils for cooking and meat chopped up into dishes rather than eaten whole.

> *"We studied the Chinese diet, and it's quite similar to the Mediterranean diet. We mix it up."*
> *Dr Timothy Kwok, Professor of Geriatric Medicine,*
> *Chinese University of Hong Kong*

In **Japan**, women live even longer than they do in Hong Kong. The life expectancy for the average female in Japan is a remarkable 88 years. And here too, diet is seen to play a key role. The Japanese diet has improved steadily in nutritional value alongside the nation's economic development. Today, the Japanese enjoy natural, unprocessed and well-balanced meals that are low in saturated fats. These mostly comprise fruit and vegetables, fish and high-grains based foods. The Japanese also tend to avoid red meat and have heeded government campaigns advising minimised salt intake. It's no wonder Japan's obesity rate is among the world's lowest.

Meanwhile, in **Italy**, another world leader in life expectancy, the Mediterranean diet is widely credited as a contributor to Italian longevity. It includes fruit and vegetables, fresh fish, olive oil, wine with meals, fewer animal fats and greater overall variety – a diet that has been linked with reduced risk of heart disease.

Taxation can be a valuable tool for discouraging the consumption of unhealthy foods. **Finland**, **Norway** and **Hungary** are among the countries that tax unhealthy foods such as confectionary, chocolate and ice cream. Besides discouraging unhealthy eating habits, such taxes also help to offset the increased costs to the healthcare system of an unhealthy citizenry. Around the world, more than 50 jurisdictions have introduced taxes on sugary drinks. In Philadelphia in the **United States**, higher taxes led consumers to reduce soft drink consumption by 22%. And in the **United Kingdom**, the initiative encouraged consumers to buy fewer soft drinks while encouraging soft drink companies to limit the sugar within the drinks. Thanks to the policy, the portion of drinks with more than five grams of sugar per 100ml fell from 49% to 15% over 3.5 years.

Promoting active lifestyles

South Africa makes physical exercise a no-brainer by providing free exercise equipment in its parks. These outdoor gyms cater to different communities, meeting the needs of children, the elderly and those with disabilities.

The **Spanish** city of Madrid has come up with a creative solution to encourage exercise among its residents, with portable gyms that can be moved to areas of greatest need. The 'cube gyms' comprise shipping containers converted into solar-powered gyms with equipment and training sessions, free of charge.

In **Brazil**, trained instructors are employed to lead free workout sessions in community spaces before and after working hours. And the same is true in **Germany** – in the city of Düsseldorf, trainers teach interested citizens 38 different types of sports and exercises including Zumba, Pilates, yoga, parkour, callisthenics and Tai Chi.

Free public exercise equipment at Haikou People's Park, China; Source: Wikimedia Commons

Meanwhile, in **Finland**, businesses spend about USD 220 annually to support each employee's physical activity, providing staff with workout facilities and gym vouchers. This benefits business productivity as well – several studies validate the positive effects of regular exercise on concentration, memory, learning, mental stamina, creativity and stress levels.

In **Sweden**, citizens are encouraged to "conquer Mount Everest" by climbing local hills and heights the equivalent number of times that would correspond to climbing the height of the world's tallest mountain. For example, going up and down the country's highest ski slope, Flottsbro, 88 times would equate to having theoretically climbed Mount Everest. Participants use an app to track their running total.

Italy has adopted a unique strategy. The country distributes boxes of 'Movement Pills' at local pharmacies, free of charge. These boxes, designed to look like typical over-the-counter medicine boxes, actually contain free 1-month coupons that citizens can use to participate in more than 1,200 sports, gyms and physical activities across the country.

In 2020, the **Romanian** city of Cluj-Napoca incentivised its residents to exercise by offering a free ride on the city's public transport network to those who completed 20 squats. A smart device would track the squats and, once completed, issue the free ticket. The initiative aimed to encourage the public to find ways to incorporate more exercise into their daily routines.

Minimising substance abuse

Tobacco is a leading cause of preventable death, killing up to half its users. And it disproportionately impacts poorer nations – more than 80% of the world's 1.3 billion tobacco users live in low- and middle-income countries.

Nations that have successfully reduced the incidence of smoking have reaped the rewards of higher life expectancies. For example, **Hong Kong** has lower rates of smoking among women compared with other parts of the world. Meanwhile, **Australia**, another top-ranking country for life expectancy, has among the lowest proportion of daily smokers among people aged 15 and over in the OECD (11%).

Norway achieved the impressive feat of increasing average citizen lifespans by *nearly four years* by reducing deaths from cardiovascular diseases. The nation effectively reduced the number of daily smokers to among the EU's lowest (from 32% to 11%) between 2000 and 2007. How did this happen? Through high taxes on tobacco products and one of the world's strictest tobacco control laws. The Norwegian Tobacco Control Act incentivises smokers to quit and disincentivises non-smokers from starting. These measures align with those the World Health Organisation has identified which reduce smoking:

- Tobacco taxes represent the most cost-effective way to decrease tobacco use and healthcare costs, especially among young people and those with low incomes. However, tax increases must be high enough to drive prices beyond income growth. In low- and middle-income countries, a 10% increase in tobacco prices reduces tobacco consumption by about 5%, whereas in high-income countries, the reduction is about 4%.
- Smoke-free laws are also effective and popular as they protect the health of non-smokers and don't harm businesses.
- Bans on promoting tobacco, including both direct (advertising on television, radio, social media, print material, billboards, etc.) and indirect forms of promotion (discounts, free distribution, point of sale displays, sponsorships, brand sharing, brand stretching, and promotions camouflaged as corporate social responsibility programmes, etc.) can reduce consumption.
- Large graphic health warnings, including packaging with powerful messages, also work.
- And the provision of professional help and evidence-based medication can more than double the chances of a person quitting.

Norway also reports one of the lowest levels of alcohol consumption and sales in Europe. Alcohol sales amount to about seven litres per person annually, compared with the EU average of ten litres. This is achieved by strict laws and policies around selling alcohol, including high taxes, a ban on advertising, strictly imposed age limits and restricted hours for selling and serving alcohol. The nation also introduced a non-profit model for distributing drinks with alcohol content over 4.75%, which are sold exclusively through the government-owned retailer Vinmonopolet.

As smoking accounts for 20-25% of all deaths in the nation, **Denmark** seeks to create a *nicotine-free generation*. It is doing so with a healthcare reform that aims to ban youth born on or after 2010 from purchasing cigarettes. The country also aims to support the more than 70% of Danish smokers who wish to adopt healthier lifestyles by promoting smoking cessation centres and programmes. The municipality of Furesø has even created a Facebook page entitled "Furesø quits smoking" including inspirational stories, gift card incentives, and more.

Iceland, another world leader for citizen lifespans, has fought teen substance abuse creatively – by combatting the highs teens sought from drugs with natural highs from sports and the arts. By increasing funding for clubs for sports, martial arts, music, dance, hip hop, etc., alongside life skills training, Iceland helped its teens reduce stress and secure a rush.

Youth enjoying a skate park; Source: PxHere

Iceland also educated parents on the importance of spending time and building relationships with their children, and encouraged them to sign agreements to take measures to protect youth, including imposing stricter rules at home and promising to keep an eye on the wellbeing of other children. Age limits were also introduced on the purchase of alcohol and on outdoor presence after midnight, and tobacco and alcohol advertising were banned.

Between 1997 and 2012, twice as many Icelandic children between 15 and 16 spent time with their parents on weekdays, while the percentage participating in organised sports at least four times a week grew from 24% to 42%. These initiatives succeeded where education on the dangers of alcohol and drugs had failed. Today, Iceland beats the rest of the EU for teens who live cleanly. The number of 15- and 16-year-olds who were drunk in the prior month dropped from 42% to 5% between 1998 and 2016. Meanwhile, those engaging in daily smoking dropped by 20%, and the percentage who had used cannabis dropped by 10%. There's evidence that the initiative reduces instances of teen suicide and crime as well.

Over in the **Czech Republic**, for a decade, the city of Prague has been encouraging residents to give up alcohol for a month every year in a campaign called 'Dry February'. Citizens are encouraged to test their control over their alcohol consumption and review its effect. Four months after the 2021 campaign, over 50% of participants reported that they had reduced their alcohol consumption, demonstrating the campaign's impact. Another Czech city, Pilsen, has banned the consumption of alcohol in several public spaces, intending to boost citizen safety, reduce vandalism and keep the streets clear of waste bottles. Among other locations, residents are not allowed to drink alcohol within 50 metres of a school or public transport facility, though they may continue to do so in restaurants and bars, at markets, cultural and sporting events.

Promoting health and hygiene

Following the collapse of the Soviet Union, **Cuba** had to find a way to feed its population. It did so by encouraging urban agriculture. The country made it free to convert unused public land into food production plots. Training in gardening was provided, and stores were opened selling compost, seeds and tools. At harvest time, food-selling permits were distributed. A decade later, about half of vegetable production across the nation was from urban gardens and farms. In Havana alone, over 30,000 people were cultivating more than 8,000 gardens – creating a healthier population.

Japan has also successfully promoted a healthy lifestyle – Japanese citizens tend to be health conscious and exercise regularly, even in old age. Indeed, the nation is known for its effective health education and deep-rooted health culture. Over time, the government has led strong public health programmes, including for tuberculosis control. Most Japanese get check-ups regularly and obtain their vaccinations and immunisations. Local government authorities conduct mass health screenings at schools, workplaces, and in the community. Business people may spend several days at hospitals or clinics to obtain thorough medical check-ups.

The Japanese are also sticklers for practising good hygiene. They benefit from a strong sanitation system and engage in regular handwashing. According to Professor Kenji Shibuya of the Department of Global Health Policy at the University of Tokyo and his colleagues, "This attitude might partly be attributable to a complex interaction of culture, education, climate, environment and the old Shinto tradition of purifying the body and mind before meeting others."

Another interesting factor seems to play a role in the adoption of healthy lifestyles – language. Some countries don't have time boundaries in their languages. For example, the economist M. Keith

Chen has explained how, while in English you may say "I will be going to a conference", in Mandarin, you would say "I go to a conference". Citizens in countries without time boundaries in their language are 30% more likely to save for retirement and 24% less likely to smoke. They also practice safer sex, exercise more often and are healthier and wealthier in retirement. This is even true within a country like **Switzerland** where people speak many different languages. It turns out that language can make the future feel closer and encourage people to act in favour of their future selves.

Technology also has a part to play. **Norway** provides citizens with free mobile applications to assist in living healthier and improving mental wellbeing. These apps tackle physical activity, adopting healthy diets, improving sleep quality, quitting smoking and reducing alcohol intake. It also provides a website that offers education on the risks of unhealthy habits and links to programmes and tips for adopting healthier behaviours.

OPTING FOR ORGAN DONATION

Organ donation saves lives. One deceased organ donor can save up to eight lives, while one tissue donor can benefit the lives of as many as 75 people.

Sri Lanka is the nation that donates the most eyes to the world. In many countries, donated corneas are in short supply – a status made worse by short shelf-life. Not so in Sri Lanka. Since the country has more donations than it needs to meet local demand, it exports corneas to restore sight in over 50 countries worldwide. Sri Lanka's Eye Donation Society reported in 2016 that one in five Sri Lankans has pledged to donate their corneas after death.

Meanwhile, **Spain** has been the world leader in organ donation for approximately 30 years. How do they achieve such high rates of donation? Their success is partly credited to a system where anyone who has not explicitly refused to donate their organs and tissues is accepted to be an organ donor once they expire. This is called an 'opt-out' system as citizens can opt out of this default process of organ donation. This is in contrast to an 'opt-in' system where citizens must actively register as organ donors to be considered for organ donation. This simple change of the default matters due to the human tendency to continue with the default option, whatever it may be.

Indeed, the use of an 'opt-out' system can dramatically improve the level of organ donation in a country. For example, despite similar cultures and levels of economic development, Germany and Austria have very different rates of organ donation. Germany, which follows an opt-in system, has an organ donation rate below 15%. Meanwhile, in Austria, where donation is the default option, over 90% of individuals donate their organs. Countries with opt-out systems save thousands of citizen lives as dramatically more donated organs are available to the people who need them.

Spain has a nationwide network for communication and transportation to enable quick extraction and transplant. It also employs carefully trained doctors to request permission from the family of the deceased – as family members can deny permission for transplants if they wish. However, despite its noble efforts, the need for organs in Spain still outstrips the number of donated organs – many patients die while on the waiting list for an organ transplant.

Other countries choose to incentivise donation. For example, in **Israel**, citizens who have signed organ donor cards are given preference in the event they have the same medical need as another person who has not chosen to donate. Since this policy was introduced in 2008, organ donation has increased – while 231 transplants occurred in 2007, the number was 433 in 2017. Israel also introduced the Brain-Respiratory Death Act in 2008, similar to the policy in Spain, where death is determined based on neurological criteria rather than heartbeat cessation, by which time organs would have begun to deteriorate and would be less viable for transplant.

Alvin Roth, professor of economics at Stanford University and Harvard University, has recommended kidney exchange programmes among living donors. This means that a person unable to donate a kidney to their loved one as they are not a match could instead donate that kidney to another person in need who has a friend or relative whose kidney *is* a match for their loved one. As a result, both individuals in need would have access to a matching kidney donor. In this way, a chain of donations could benefit many recipients. In fact, there has even been an instance of a chain of 70 such donations! This concept boosts the availability of kidneys, though unfortunately, it cannot come close to meeting the demand.

Iran is the only country which has cleared its waiting list for kidney donation. It achieved this by being the only country to pay kidney donors – a practice condemned by the World Health Organisation as it is deemed to exploit vulnerable members of society. Countries like Singapore and Australia do allow limited payments to organ donors, but primarily as compensation for lost working time. However, since adopting its system of payment in 1988, the number of transplants in Iran nearly doubled within a year and, within 11 years, the country was able to eliminate the shortage of kidney donors. The government sets a fixed price of USD 4,600 per organ and matches buyers and sellers. The Kidney Foundation of Iran or charitable organisations may help cover costs for recipients unable to pay.

Though the practice of paying organ donors is widely criticised, Nobel Laureate economist Gary Becker recommends it, citing the growing waiting times and many thousands of deaths associated with systems dependent on deaths and altruistic donations. Indeed, the number of patients on the United States' transplant list has grown from fewer than 25,000 in the early 1990s to over 100,000 today, and 17 people die waiting each day. The majority of organ donations result from car crashes, which means that when driving improves or pandemics keep people indoors, organ donation dwindles. Becker estimates that a payment of approximately USD 15,000 for living donors would alleviate the shortage of kidneys in the United States.

MAKING AGEING EASY

Enabling active ageing

Creating age-friendly cultures and environments seems to hold a clue to maximising lifespans. In frontrunner **Hong Kong**, most districts are categorised as "age-friendly cities". Walking to open markets, shops, malls, and other places is easy. The streets are safe with ready access to public transport, affordable taxis, many active amenities like parks and trails, and healthy food. The metro is clean and air-conditioned, and a ride starts at only USD 0.60. Seniors regularly engage in morning exercise, even in urban environments, and walking routes can be easily accessed with the help of footbridges and elevators. By considering age and handicaps in the design of most spaces, the environment empowers seniors with more personal control over their lives and activities. The culture also promotes positive images of the elderly, and they engage in active leisure and spiritual wellbeing programmes.

The Nordic countries are also consistently ranked among the best countries in which to grow old. **Finland** provides free gym facilities for those over 65. This benefits both seniors and the country, as fit elders require less medical care. The Finnish capital, Helsinki, has also invested in arts and culture activities for its seniors with about USD 1.3 million in grants made available for projects catering to the elderly in the spaces of music, film, dance, theatre, circus, handicrafts and visual arts.

Intellectual stimulation is also available in **Italy**, where the city of Genoa has had, since 1983, a 'University of the Third Age' providing courses to individuals over 45 on everything from art history to medicine to economics. The university offers the retired population mental engagement and opportunities for connection. The city also provides a free, on-call bus service for residents over the age of 65, empowering seniors to stay active, perform errands and socialise. Similarly, in the city of Athens in **Greece**, 25 'friendship clubs' enable the city's senior citizens to meet new people. Here, they engage in sports, excursions, mental health support groups and cultural events, and learn new skills, such as how to use digital devices.

Meanwhile, in the **Polish** capital, Warsaw, businesses are being supported in continuing to employ seniors as the city provides training and covers part of their salaries. This helps companies build multigenerational teams that can withstand labour shortages as the population ages, while enabling seniors to make use of their skills and actively fill their free time. **Japan**, too, offers a 'Second Life' scheme which employs seniors in part-time jobs such as working at the local kindergarten, to keep retirees occupied and engaged in the community.

Rotterdam in the **Netherlands** is making efforts to deliver digital learning to its retirees. Here, young 'Digicoaches' volunteer to provide free phone, web and email support to people over 55 in the language of the senior's preference. Over in **France**, a caravan is travelling around the Bouches-du-Rhône region, visiting people over 60 and providing them with digital education and help in performing online activities.

Besides laptop training and individual support with specific devices, relaxing virtual reality experiences are also introduced to help with psychological wellbeing. And there's more to come. In the future, adapted tablets with a simplified interface and large characters will also be lent to seniors, with a 4G package included.

Facilitating independent living

In **Norway** and **Sweden**, as in **Germany** and the **Netherlands**, the municipality supports ageing citizens in remaining in their own homes for as long as possible. It does so by providing home health aides, food delivery, house cleaning and shopping services, either for free or at an affordable price. Seniors are empowered to make choices – municipalities can provide a home help aid to step in on weekends or over a vacation period. Often, a stipend is available to those who stay home to care for an ailing loved one. Similarly, in **South Korea**, relatives living with disabled family members are now registered and paid as temporary care workers.

The city of Rotterdam in the **Netherlands** is actively introducing its senior citizens to technologies that can support them in living independently for longer with 'Comfort Houses' where volunteers set up and demonstrate assistive devices in a model home environment. The most popular products include a digital doorbell with video, remote-controlled curtains, a toilet dryer, an electric drying rack, a robot cat/dog, a talking alarm clock, a smart home speaker and a robot vacuum cleaner. Seniors can also borrow products to test at home.

The **Polish** city of Gliwice offers residents over the age of 60 a monthly repair service, enabling seniors who live alone to access plumbing, carpentry, lock repair and electrical services. The city budget subsidises the costs. The city of Lodz is also making efforts to connect its elderly residents with needed services – with a smart wristband that tracks the wearer's vitals and notifies relatives and emergency services in case of major health risks. Besides heart rate, body temperature and physical activity, the wristband can also detect a fall.

Meanwhile, in Ghent in **Belgium**, a 'yellow box' programme aims to help save seniors' lives. The initiative involves storing personal and medical information about the individual inside a yellow box placed in the fridge, then placing a sticker on the inside of the front door – so that paramedics know they can quickly locate needed information in the event of an emergency. Boxes are made available for free via pharmacies and local service centres.

In **Norway** and **Sweden**, the expenses of moving into assisted living facilities are partially covered by pension funds, while the rest is funded by the public system. Seniors can also opt to move into private assisted living facilities. **Germany** and the **Netherlands** also have dedicated financing in place for long-term care.

Providing the elderly with independence is a critical ingredient for boosting life satisfaction. In his book 'Being Mortal', Dr Atul Gawande stresses that older people should be provided with choices in what they do. This can mean having a lockable door, the ability to dress oneself, wake and sleep when one wants, choose furnishings and decide whether to keep pets or have someone over to stay the night. He highlights the importance of not confining choices in the name of safety, but expanding them in the name of living a more fulfilling life.

Filling life with living things

Seniors in **Hong Kong** benefit from the close familial ties often found among Asian cultures, as well as a philosophy of respect for parents, elders and ancestors. The wellbeing of older family members is prioritised, providing crucial social, psychological, physical and financial support. Where individuals cannot physically attend to older loved ones, they extend support through video calls and cash transfers. In

Japan too, the importance of community support is recognised, and seniors can join groups to stay active and keep in touch with their neighbours.

Dr Gawande shares case studies of living facilities that strive to fill their spaces with life. The Eden Alternative, an international non-profit, designs assisted living facilities that are strategically filled with plants, animals and children. This serves seniors by attacking feelings of boredom (by providing interest and entertainment), loneliness (by providing companionship), and helplessness (by requiring care). For example, the Newridge assisted care facility shares its grounds with a preschool, which organises common programmes and shared activities. Research confirms that even looking after a plant can add immensely to the quality of life of an older person. Dr Bill Thomas, the visionary behind The Eden Alternative, describes how he planned to put rabbits, two dogs, four cats, and a hundred birds into an assisted living facility, with live plants and bird cages in every room. The facility also provided on-site care to children, complete with a playground. The outcome of these efforts was a remarkable 15% decline in deaths among the resident elders.

Another assisted living facility lauded by Dr Thomas houses residents in separate rooms around one shared living area. A sense of privacy and community is created by limiting the living area to no more than 20 people. Meanwhile, open areas allow people to see what others are up to and to join in. Dr Thomas benchmarks small, communal homes with no more than 12 residents – warm and homey spaces with a doorbell, informal furniture and family-style meals around a big table.

Other countries have also made an effort to integrate youth and seniors – for the wellbeing of both. For example, **Sweden** has flats that can be rented only by either pensioners *or* under-25-year-olds, with the requirement that they spend at least 2 hours a week together.

3
Education
Grooming Utopian generations

"Education is the most powerful weapon
to change the world."
Nelson Mandela, first president of South Africa

It is almost universally accepted that education systems around the world need a major overhaul. Naturally, Utopia would feature an incredible education system – with the power to shape youth minds and attitudes in a transformative way and lay the foundation for a glowing future. But where should we look for inspiration?

Since 2000, one country has been in the limelight for the quality of its education system, consistently ranking as a leader in primary, secondary and tertiary education. That country is **Finland**. Indeed, when GDP is adjusted for, the higher education system of Finland stands out as the world's best, as shown in the 2020 Universitas 21 rankings, which compare countries' higher education systems rather than the merits and drawbacks of particular universities. According to the authors, these rankings provide clues on how nations can improve educational outcomes. Ross Williams, professor at Melbourne Institute, explains: "Good outcomes require resources and appropriate government policies. Together these factors explain three-quarters of the variation in outcomes."

MAXIMISING EVERY STUDENT'S SUCCESS

Providing free education

Since the 1980s, **Finland** has strived to use education to balance out social inequity. In fact, equal access to education is a constitutional right. Education is free at all levels, including college and graduate programmes, which are free for anyone accepted into the programme, including foreign students. In Finland, only books, transportation and school supplies need to be paid for, with student financial aid available if needed. Students also get free school meals and access to healthcare, counselling and personalised guidance.

Estonia, a country which topped the 2018 PISA rankings of global education systems, also provides free education, including textbooks and cafeteria meals. And debt-free education is present in **Denmark** too, another global benchmark in education. And it does make a difference. For contrast, the average student in the United States graduates with a debt of around USD 30,000. The need to pay off this debt can lead students into careers that do not align with what they have studied or to stay with jobs that they dislike. Graduating debt-free, on the other hand, empowers students to take more risks and grow in the fields where they feel most engaged.

Emphasising individualised learning

If you visit a classroom in **Finland**, you aren't likely to see students being lectured by a teacher. Here is what you might see students doing instead:

- Working with their teachers to set their own weekly subject targets and deciding what to do to meet them
- Walking around, collecting information, popping into workshops, asking questions from their teacher, engaging in problem-solving and performing evaluations
- Working on individual projects or small group projects

Such independent and active work helps students build the skills to spot, grapple with and effectively solve problems, evaluate and improve themselves, and learn proactively. Rather than expecting information to be fed to them, students are actively involved in their own learning journeys.

Meanwhile, Finnish teachers develop almost familial understandings of their students as they usually work with the same class of about 19 pupils for up to six years. This builds mutual trust, respect and bonding, letting teachers become coaches and mentors catering to each student's unique goals, needs and learning styles.

"If a child can't learn the way we teach,
maybe we should teach the way they learn."
Ignacio Estrada, educational consultant

Eliminating tests

There are no standardised tests in **Finland**. Instead, students are graded in a personalised way according to a grading system determined by their teacher. This approach bypasses a "teaching to the test" environment in schools, prioritising genuine learning over cramming to secure test results. To track overall progress, the Ministry of Education samples groups across different ranges of schools.

In fact, there is only one test in Finland and it can be voluntarily taken upon completing high school. This test is typically based on specialities that the student has developed while in school. It also readily addresses complex, even controversial, topics. Pasi Sahlberg, a professor and former director general at the Finland Ministry of Education, describes some usual questions: "In what sense are happiness, good life and wellbeing ethical concepts?" "Karl Marx and Friedrich Engels predicted that a socialist revolution would first happen in countries like Great Britain. What made Marx and Engels claim that and why did a socialist revolution happen in Russia?" Needless to say, these tests are graded by teachers, not computers.

Respecting diverse fields

In **Finland**, priority is given to *both* university and vocational education. Upon completing school, Finnish students can choose to follow a three-year vocational programme to gain training for a specific career. Finnish vocational education is well respected, with 40% of Finns enrolling after their basic education. An impressive 90% feel that it offers high-quality learning.

Finland also values artists and has provided them with grants and subsidies since 1969. These tax-free monthly stipends benefit artists engaged in architecture, crafts, dance, design, literature, video, music, theatre, photography and more. The government often purchases artworks to enliven public buildings and spaces.

Denmark has a unique model for offering individualised education, with 74 Danish folk schools providing an active liberal arts education. Around 60,000 Danes attend annually, and there are no academic requirements for admittance. Classes are based on dialogue and mutual learning between teachers and students, and there are no grades or exams. Instead, programmes are characterised by the free word and an open curriculum which can be altered during the course. The schools are boarding schools, so the mostly 18- to 24-year-old students sleep, eat, study, and spend their spare time at the school. Most pupils stay for about four months. The schools aim to uncover and develop each student's unique skills in a challenging but supportive social atmosphere.

Dan Buettner of National Geographic suggests that Denmark's unique model of folk schools could be contributing to the country's high levels of happiness. How? By enabling the creation of the 'flow' state in their students. The 'flow' state, first described by psychologist Mihalyi Csikszentmihalyi, is an authentically happy state of engagement. It is usually experienced while doing something that one finds both pleasing and sufficiently challenging to fully occupy oneself. By providing students with the freedom to explore subjects of interest to them at their own pace, these schools deliver an environment that produces pleasurable striving.

"The Danes seem more aware of the
total needs of a person than most other places."
Mihaly Csikszentmihalyi, psychologist

Preparing for bright futures

As of 2022, **Estonia** has the highest proportion of entrepreneurs of any European country. Each year, more than 20 companies are created for every 1,000 inhabitants – six times higher than the EU average! In fact, the Estonian education system is geared to make this possible. Academic programmes are designed with involvement from companies and civil society, so they address real-world problems. Meanwhile, both secondary and tertiary education, whether vocational or academic, includes work placements. These can account for up to half of the required training hours. As a result, Estonian youth already have work experience under their belts before they even enter the labour market.

Over in the **Latvian** city of Jelgava, from the age of 16, youth are empowered to make informed decisions by sampling careers before they embark on them. Internship placements are encouraged in several fields, including medicine and pharmacy, IT technologies, trade and logistics, catering, construction, education and psychology. Latvian youth also benefit from group career counselling, self-knowledge exercises, and the chance to draw up personalised career plans.

VALUING AND TRAINING TEACHERS

In **Finland**, teaching is a highly respected profession. This is often credited as the key factor that led its education system to climb from mediocrity to world leadership.

Most Finnish teachers have master's degrees in both education *and* their subject area. In fact, a master's degree is a must to enter the field and the rigorous teaching schools are highly selective – only about one in 10 applicants are admitted. Selected teachers follow a graduate-level teacher preparation programme over three years. The programme is free and participants are even provided with a living stipend while they are in the programme.

As part of their training, teachers learn to create challenging curricula and performance assessments that lead students to critically question and research subject areas. There is coursework on how to teach, with priority given to the latest research, and a minimum of one year of practical training in a model school where innovative teaching practices are emphasised. Inclusivity in terms of culture, learning styles and special needs is emphasised. This ensures that no child will be denied an opportunity to learn.

With their combined knowledge of both research and educational methodologies, teachers in Finland are clever diagnosticians. The value of empowering teachers in this way has been neatly summed up by a Finnish official, who said: "Professional teachers should have space for innovation because they should try to find new ways to improve learning. Teachers should not be seen as technicians whose work is to implement strictly dictated syllabi, but rather as professionals who know how to improve learning for all. Teachers are ranked highest in importance because educational systems work through them."

"There's no word for accountability in Finnish… Accountability is something that is left
when responsibility has been subtracted."
Pasi Sahlberg, former director of the
Finnish Ministry of Education

In **Estonia** too, 83% of school principals (nearly double the OECD average of 42%) say teachers play an important role in tasks like designing school policies, the curriculum and teaching methods.

The **Finnish** teaching environment is not a competitive one. In a setting free from teacher and school rankings and ratings, cooperation is normal. Schools are encouraged to share resources, and teachers collaborate to develop curricula. They also engage in groups for problem-solving, following a process of planning, action and evaluation – similar to the methodology they will help their students practice.

Teachers also get time for professional development, with nearly half their time in school devoted to honing their practice. This includes curriculum work, planning alongside other teachers, and collaborating with parents. As Pasi Sahlberg, former director of the Finnish Ministry of Education, says: "Finnish teachers are conscious, critical consumers of professional development and in-service training services. Continuous upgrading of teachers' pedagogical professionalism has become a right rather than an obligation."

Respecting and enabling teachers is a key ingredient driving Finland's success. Finnish teachers are treated like university professors. Compared to their counterparts in the United States, they teach for fewer hours and are paid slightly more (USD 41,000 a year in the US versus USD 43,000 in Finland).

REMOVING STRESS FROM LEARNING

Another noticeable difference within **Finland**'s education system is that it's a lot more relaxed. It is not about stuffing children with facts, but patiently creating lifelong learners. In Finland, there are only nine compulsory years of schooling. Finnish children only start attending school at the age of seven – and they are free to stop at the age of 16.

They also start the day later than the rest of the world – usually between 9:00 am and 9:45 am. This aligns with research that shows that early starts interrupt children's natural sleep cycles and harm their wellbeing and development. The school day usually wraps up between 2:00 pm and 2:45 pm.

Finnish schools typically have only a few classes per day, long periods and frequent breaks. By law, students are entitled to 15-minute breaks after every 45 minutes, allowing them to walk around, stretch, have a snack, pop outdoors, relax and unwind. The result is an environment where learning is enjoyable, holistic and healthy. By comparison, students in the United States usually get less than half an hour of recess each day. Psychologist and research professor Peter Gray suggests that this 'play deficit' could increase anxiety and other mental health concerns.

"One test of the correctness of educational procedure is the happiness of the child."
Maria Montessori, Italian physician and educator

Finnish students also spend far less time on homework, with the OECD reporting that they have the least outside work and homework of all nations worldwide. While students in the United States spend over six hours a week on homework, students in Finland spend about 2.8 hours. They also don't have tutors. Instead, Finnish kids spend more time engaged in activities like sports. In 2020, more than 80% of 10-year-olds in Finland's capital, Helsinki, participated in sports activities outside school.

Other countries are also making efforts to make schools more relaxed environments. In Turin, **Italy**, children enjoy 'nature classrooms' where they can engage in open-air learning among ponds, flower beds and tall trees.

Meanwhile, the **Polish** city of Wroclaw has adopted a special way of keeping classroom stress levels low – by inviting children's furry friends in. Well-behaved pets may spend time in the classroom and library, where a librarian commented that the kids are happier – and also borrowing more books!

PRIORITISING CHARACTER DEVELOPMENT

Cultivating life skills

> *"Intelligence plus character –*
> *that is the goal of true education."*
> Martin Luther King Jr., civil rights activist

Around the world, more and more countries and schools are appreciating that the role of education has changed. Education used to be largely about transferring facts and trivia from teachers and books to students. In a post-Internet world, where information is readily available, education can serve a fresh purpose. For many countries, this purpose is to develop students' character and critical thinking skills.

In **Finland**, the national curriculum includes the development of crucial life skills, incorporated across all subjects for grades 1-9. The core competence areas emphasised are:

- thinking and learning to learn
- taking care of oneself and managing daily life
- interaction and expression
- cultural competence
- multi-literacy
- working life competence and entrepreneurship
- technology competence
- participation, involvement and building a sustainable future

Topics include developing and justifying views, child rights and responsibilities, friendship, positive class and school society formation, and preventing discrimination. Issues like equality, conflict management, stress and crisis, and responsible decision-making are also tackled, as well as emotion expression and regulation. At the upper secondary level, students can more deeply study skills on understanding emotions, taking responsibility, persisting and self-managing, as well as cultivating social relationships and practising empathy, cooperation, amiability and assertiveness.

Such school-based social and emotional learning programmes significantly benefit students' skills. They have been shown to improve children's perceptions of themselves, other people and school, while boosting school performance, increasing helpful behaviour and reducing behavioural issues.

"Students are regularly asked to show their ability to cope with issues related to evolution, losing a job, dieting, political issues, violence, war, ethics in sports, junk food, sex, drugs, and popular music. Such issues span across subject areas and often require multi-disciplinary knowledge and skills."
Pasi Sahlberg, former director of the Finnish Ministry of Education

Countries in Asia are also taking steps to boost character building. In **Singapore**, the curriculum emphasises nurturing "21st century competencies" to develop confident, active contributors who are self-directed learners and concerned citizens. Accordingly, the curriculum seeks to develop skills in critical and inventive thinking, communication, collaboration, and information, civic literacy, global awareness, and cross-cultural skills. **Hong Kong** also emphasises "whole-person education" focusing on responsibility, respect for others, perseverance, commitment, integrity, national identity, and care for others. In primary school, self-concept, interpersonal relationships, values, and attitudes towards school are emphasised, while in secondary school, topics of health and wellbeing, stress management, life goals, leadership, ethics and global citizenship are added. Meanwhile, in **Japan**, socio-emotional skills are prioritised to develop a "zest for life" among students.

Finland also takes bullying seriously. The country has launched a national anti-bullying programme which includes conversations around bullying, respect, and working in a group, and involves activities and group work. A computer game complements the programme, featuring a virtual school where children can practice preventing bullying by demonstrating support for a maltreated classmate. The year-long programme also includes interventions for youth who have engaged in bullying. Meanwhile, online surveys completed by students and staff provide the school with information to support their efforts to stamp out bullying.

Gamification is also used in Rotterdam in the **Netherlands**, where children can play a free computer game called HackShield. They act as cyber agents, learn about cybercrime such as hacking, phishing and misinformation, and protect themselves and their family and friends from the phenomena, gaining shields at each level. The game teaches children valuable skills for navigating an increasingly digital world.

Building independence outside school

Cultivating independence and a sense of responsibility in youth reaps long-term rewards. In **Denmark**, children are given autonomy and treated independently from a young age. For example, six-year-olds might be given an equal say in how household expenses are budgeted and where the family will take their vacations. This teaches youth that they have both influence and responsibility.

"The great aim of education is not knowledge but action."
Herbert Spencer, English philosopher and sociologist

Helsinki, the capital of **Finland**, operates many city-level activities to engage young people in community participation. The goal is to see that every youth has at least one experience annually of making a difference. Here are some examples:

- The Youth Council is a youth lobbying body comprising 30 young people aged 13 to 17, elected every two years. Established by municipal law, the council aims to see that youth have a voice in decision-making about city activities.
- Via a dedicated website, youth can submit proposals to the City of Helsinki for initiatives that would boost collective wellbeing. For example, requesting a basketball court in their neighbourhood or benches for a park near their school, or flagging an unsafe intersection in their area.
- Children may generate ideas, vote and negotiate on what leisure activities and facilities will be made available to Helsinki's youth each year. Those aged 7 to 28 may apply for and obtain grants to implement projects and ideas.
- Youth are encouraged to form school groups to address issues of importance to them, such as the environment or wellbeing.
- Student councils are assigned funds to help improve school camaraderie or the study environment.

Similarly, in **Switzerland**, a Youth Parliament representing those between 12-30 years of age has submitted about 150 petitions annually to the Swiss authorities since being founded in 1991. The petitions are the result of formal deliberations by 200 members at an annual youth session in the House of Representatives.

4
Environment
A clean, green living space

"The Earth is a fine place and worth fighting for."
Ernest Hemingway, American novelist

Needless to say, the Utopian environment must be eco-friendly and pollutant-free, featuring renewable energy sources and waste-free living. But, is this a pipe dream? Luckily, a few countries – from **Bhutan** to **Denmark** – hold the clues to making such an environment a reality.

Let's explore the nations that are removing carbon dioxide from the world, exporting renewable energy, growing their economies even while reducing their energy use, and empowering citizens to lead green lifestyles.

ACTIVELY REDUCING EMISSIONS

As of 2017, **Bhutan** was the only country that was carbon neutral, a term used to describe a state of balance between carbon emissions and carbon removal. Indeed, the nation is not just carbon neutral, but carbon negative. This means it is in the highly unusual position of absorbing more carbon from the atmosphere than it releases.

Bhutan has made this possible with a constitution that demands that at least 60% of the country's landmass shall remain under forest cover *for all time*. In 1999, the nation even banned logging exports. As a result of these efforts, the country generates 2.2 million tons of carbon dioxide, but its forests sequester more than three times that amount, making Bhutan a net carbon sink eliminating millions of tons of carbon dioxide each year. For comparison, Luxembourg produces four times as much carbon dioxide despite having a smaller population than Bhutan.

*"When we destroy something created by man,
we call it vandalism. When we destroy something
created by nature, we call it progress."*
Ed Begley Jr., American actor and environmental activist

In its efforts to remain carbon neutral, Bhutan has provided free electricity to rural farmers so they need not use firewood to cook. It has invested in sustainable transport and subsidised the purchase of electric vehicles and LED lights. The entire government even established a plan to go paperless. Meanwhile, national programmes like Clean Bhutan and Green Bhutan involve nationwide clean-up and tree-planting efforts. In fact, Bhutan has claimed world records for planting the most trees per hour. Today, the nations of **Suriname** and **Panama** have also followed suit in protecting forest cover and becoming carbon negative.

In 1972, **Denmark** drew up the Stockholm Declaration – the first document to recognise access to a clean environment as a fundamental human right. And the Scandinavian nation is maintaining its lead. In 2020, Denmark pledged to end oil and gas exploration by 2050 and reinvest those funds towards retraining people for jobs in green technology.

It was the **United Kingdom** that first introduced long-term climate targets into national law. The government is legally committed to achieving net zero carbon emissions by 2050. **Sweden** has followed suit and gone further, making it legally binding for the nation to be carbon neutral by 2045. Meanwhile, the European Parliament is tackling a major source of emissions. It has made it mandatory for European airlines to introduce sustainable aviation fuel from 2025 onwards – to make up 85% of the industry's fuel mix by 2050.

Taxes also have a part to play. Research affirms that charging companies for carbon emissions via a fee or tax effectively reduces greenhouse gas emissions and pollution. In 2006, California in the **United States** required companies to pay for their carbon emissions. The state set a limit on emissions, then progressively lowered that limit in the following years. Companies that did not reduce their pollution had to pay for carbon allowances. The initiative led to a significant reduction in emissions even while the state's economy grew by 12%, exceeding the national average.

CHOOSING RENEWABLE ENERGY

Committing to renewables

1980 saw **Denmark** achieve the impressive feat of making its economic growth independent from its total energy consumption. While Danish GDP has doubled, its emissions have halved, its energy consumption remains largely unchanged, and water consumption has plummeted by 40%. Denmark has pledged that, by 2030, it will cut its emissions to 70%

of what they were in 1990 and become completely independent of fossil fuels.

How has Denmark made this happen? By transitioning to renewable energy – about 70% of electricity in the nation comes from renewables, including 25% from wind turbines. Denmark has financed the transition through public-private partnerships, and citizens can invest with shared ownership. Residents also pay a carbon tax of around USD 13 per ton of carbon dioxide. The nation has even announced plans to construct an artificial island to house a massive wind farm in the North Sea that would provide energy to Denmark and its neighbours.

The renewable energy system in Denmark is also highly efficient. The water and electricity sectors collaborate, making use of sludge from wastewater treatment plants to produce energy. Meanwhile, excess heat from electricity production is used by the district heating system. And waste from citizens in cities is made use of to generate heat and electricity.

Indeed, all the Nordic countries are known for their use of renewable energy. While Denmark is renowned for wind energy, Norway is known for hydroelectricity, Iceland for geothermal energy, and Finland and Sweden for bioenergy. Virtually all of the electricity in **Iceland** is generated from renewable hydropower and geothermal energy sources. The trade of electricity among the Nordic and European integrated electricity market is a key factor that ensures a secure supply of renewables to each nation.

Bhutan, meanwhile, produces so much hydroelectricity that it exports most of the renewable electricity generated from its fast-flowing rivers. This offsets about six million tons of carbon dioxide in the region as of 2016, and the nation plans to export much more clean green energy.

Other countries are also making their way towards a sustainable future. In **Germany**, over 10 years, all states will have to allocate a portion of their land to wind turbines. The country is striving to become greenhouse gas neutral by 2050.

Engaging citizens to produce clean energy

Austria is involving its citizens in the green transition. In Vienna, 'citizen-solar power plants' have been around for a decade. More than 10,000 citizens have collectively invested over USD 38 million in solar energy parks that power over 8,400 households and save 12,000 tons of carbon emissions annually.

And in the Austrian city of Dornbirn, citizens were given the chance to invest in the placement of solar panels on public buildings such as schools, kindergartens and fire stations. They could invest about USD 500 to purchase a share in the project, with the city offering about USD 600 worth of grocery vouchers in return, paid out over 10 years. The nearly 500 shares made available were sold in just 10 days.

> *"There are no passengers on spaceship Earth.*
> *We are all crew."*
> *Marshall McLuhan, Canadian philosopher*

An Austrian company founded in the late 1800s, Energie AG, is empowering citizens to get involved in the solar movement. The company has introduced an app to support citizens in Upper Austria in sharing excess energy from their private solar panels. The solar power producers can set the price for their excess electricity and other app users can buy from them at the stated price. On gloomy days when the sun does not shine, Energie AG meets the demand for electricity at the standard price. In 2020, enough solar power systems were set up in the region to account for a quarter of the growth in renewable energy sources across the nation.

The mayor of the Austrian town of Stanz im Mürztal is even planning that its residents will be able to track their solar energy production on an app and swap excess energy for grocery products at the store.

In **Bulgaria**, the city of Burgas is supporting citizens in installing solar roofs with a digital platform. The tool can calculate every building's potential solar energy output as well as the cost of installation. It takes into account the orientation of each building towards the sun and calculates how many panels can be installed based on roof size.

Luxembourg is also encouraging residents to view solar panels as a lucrative investment – using tax incentives. In 2021, the country made the sale of solar energy within 10 kilowatt-peaks tax-free. Similarly, **Italy** is offering people, cooperatives and condominiums a 110% tax deduction on expenses for interventions related to energy efficiency, solar system installation and electric vehicle charging infrastructure.

Meanwhile, in **Spain**, the city of Valencia is supporting the creation of 'energy communities' – neighbourhoods that freely share renewable energy. The city hopes to see 100 such communities emerge within its borders.

ENCOURAGING GREEN LIFESTYLES

Boosting electric vehicle use

Norway is a world leader in conscious commuting, with a whopping 75% of vehicle buyers having chosen electric vehicles in 2020 – the most in the world. Why are Norwegians so keen to go electric? It isn't by accident. Norway imposes heavy car registration taxes and vehicle import duties. By waiving these for electric vehicles, and introducing other incentives like toll exemptions and free parking facilities with charging ports, citizens are encouraged to go electric.

The country with the second-highest electric vehicle adoption rate in 2020 was **Iceland**, at 45%. Iceland has been laying the foundation for eco-friendly transport for decades with a combination of renewable energy, high fossil fuel prices, low electricity prices and a high degree of urbanisation. Like Norway, Iceland can use 100% renewable energy in powering its electric vehicles.

Other countries and cities are taking steps as well. Hamburg in **Germany** and Madrid in **Spain** have both banned older diesel vehicles from their roads as these vehicles are key emission offenders. Meanwhile, since 2009, **Brazil**'s city of Curitiba uses only energy-efficient biofuel buses and hybrid electric/biofuel buses. These cut back emissions by more than 25% compared with conventional buses. And over in **Austria**, the vehicle fleet of the Viennese municipality will go entirely electric from 2025.

In Berlin, **Germany**, citizens are being supported in charging electric vehicles – with 1,000 street lamps targeted to double as charging points. In Frankfurt, car parks feature charging stations to allow citizens to refuel while their car is parked. And in the **Danish** municipality of Frederiksberg, over 95% of residents live less than 250 metres from a charging point.

Another approach to minimising vehicle emissions is cutting back on unnecessary trips. The city of Miami in the **United States** uses artificial intelligence to assess whether city dumpsters are full. If they are not, municipal dump trucks are notified and can avoid unnecessary trips to empty the half-filled dumpsters.

Promoting public transport

Another way to turn citizens away from energy-inefficient car use is with effective public transport. The city of Curitiba in **Brazil** has a rapid transit system for buses that is so good it has been replicated in over 300 countries. The system, used for 70-80% of daily trips in the city, is popular thanks to its cheap and standard ticket prices (a single fare of about USD 0.40 for the whole network), dedicated express lanes that ensure fast travel, and elevated bus stations which enable quick boarding.

Other cities discourage car use with free public transport. The **French** city of Aubagne has been doing so since 2009 and introduced the world's first free tram network. In three years, it removed 5,000 cars from the roads, a 10% reduction, and made public transport 235% more popular. And in 2020, **Luxembourg** became the first country in the world to provide free public transport.

In the municipality of Cascais in **Portugal**, 10% more commuters are choosing to use public transport since it was made free two years ago. The free service is paid for by car users who pay parking fees at municipality car parks and through taxes levied on those who use individual transport. Beyond Cascais, in the city of Lisbon, public transport is free to students under 23 and those over 65.

Other countries have also been taking steps to promote public transport. For example, the **Romanian** city of Cluj-Napoca practices "Green Fridays", encouraging citizens to leave their vehicles at home and use free public transport on Fridays. Meanwhile, the **Spanish** region of Valencia offers free public transport on Sundays, while Madrid and Barcelona have offered commuters four months of free train travel. In the **Czech** city of Pilsen, a new car park has cropped up near a major transport terminal. The parking ticket (about USD 2.5) doubles as an all-day public transport pass. The goal is to encourage travellers to park their cars and use public transport within the city.

In 2021, **France** unveiled the world's lowest energy-per-kilometre rail vehicle called the UrbanLoop, set to debut in the public transport system in 2026. The system involves electric transportation of individual pods – unexpectedly more energy efficient than mass transit. A predictive algorithm sends pods to sites of greatest demand and stops occur on a separate line to prevent congestion. Individual pods use energy from the rails and can communicate with each other to ensure they don't collide.

Greening grocery shopping

"'It's only one straw', said 8 billion people."
Anonymous

Three communities in California in the **United States** are effectively tackling plastic waste – with the simple initiative of charging 10 cents for a plastic bag. They have found that while 75% of people will use a free plastic bag to carry their items, that percentage drops to 16% when the bag costs 10 cents. The minor fee makes people think twice about whether they really need a bag, and remember to bring their own. Communities across the country have started to adopt this simple policy.

Other nations are banning PVC plastic altogether, as **South Korea** did in 2019 and **Taiwan** is scheduled to do in 2023. By 2025, the use of most single-use plastics will be banned in **New Zealand** as well.

In Sofia, **Bulgaria**, an interactive online map was introduced to reduce the purchase of single-use plastic water bottles. The map, which can be found at zerowastesofia.com/watermap, depicts every public water fountain or restaurant where citizens can refill their water bottles for free.

Meanwhile, **Denmark** is shining a spotlight on the environmental impact of various foods. In 2022, it became the first country to introduce a government-controlled climate label that gives consumers insights into whether food has been produced with consideration of the environment in mind.

Supporting low-emission diets

Given that animal farming is a major contributor to deforestation and results in more greenhouse gas emissions than all forms of transport combined, minimising meat and dairy consumption is arguably the single biggest way to reduce environmental impact. Some cities are taking the lead in promoting the reduction of meat consumption. The largest school district in the **United States**, serving over 1.1 million students, New York City introduced Meatless Mondays in all its public schools in 2019. For one day each week, all cafeteria food (which includes breakfast and lunch) is vegetarian. The initiative, an effort to curb New Yorkers' greenhouse gas emissions and improve public health, began as a pilot programme in 15 schools. It proved to be cost-efficient and welcomed by students. The city found that younger people tend to embrace plant-based diets more readily and are often highly concerned about climate change. Over 100 other districts across the United States have also elected to adopt the policy. And in 2022, Vegan Fridays were introduced to all New York City public schools.

Meanwhile, in the municipality of Salvador in **Brazil**, a 2022 programme aims to make 10 million school meals healthier and more eco-friendly by replacing meats with vegetables, fruits, grains and legumes. The goal is to improve students' health while protecting the environment and animal welfare.

Championing sustainable living

Finland has created a website offering its citizens a simple yet comprehensive guide to reducing their carbon footprint. The beautifully illustrated website (hiilihelppi.fi) allows users to learn best practices based on the type of home they live in. Among a range of topics, citizens can learn about urban farming, green roofs, spatial efficiency, and even how they can influence environmental decision-making in their neighbourhood.

The **Spanish** province of Gipuzkoa also activated its citizenry, with a six-month competition in 2021 inviting individual municipalities to compete to boost citizen sustainability across seven categories: energy, food, mobility, waste, water consumption, textiles and biodiversity. Those municipalities that achieved the first three places, as tracked on an app, were awarded cash prizes of about USD 40,000, 20,000 and 10,000 to invest in their municipality as they wished. An impressive 85% of residents reported that they had taken action to combat climate change, including separating garbage, avoiding single-use items, buying efficient appliances and opting to purchase locally. Individuals who secured the most points were rewarded with vouchers for the use of electric vehicles and other incentives.

Sweden is taking things further by setting up 'sharing cities'. These cities make use of the sharing economy to enable people to own less but have more. Commonly used spaces and items, including gardens, tools, clothing, toys, vehicles, etc., are made available for common use, minimising the need for individual families to own them exclusively. Many participants find that this saves cost and space while promoting community relations and benefitting the environment.

"Consume less; share better."
Hervé Kempf, French journalist and writer

'Libraries of Things' are becoming increasingly popular around the world. In Philadelphia in the **United States**, the West Philly Tool Library allows individuals and organisations to borrow equipment so they need not purchase it. Tools for gardening, plumbing, cleaning, carpentry and more are available to borrow, often at no cost beyond the nominal library membership fee. Training to use the tools is also provided.

Meanwhile, Barcelona in **Spain** is supporting its residents in reducing their carbon footprint when they fly. An online platform allows passengers to review their individual carbon footprint of their next flight and pay the difference to replace the kerosene fuel required for their travel with sustainable aviation fuel. Passengers can decide the extent to which they want to contribute to making their flight eco-friendly and the corresponding amount of biofuel is then delivered to the airport.

FOSTERING A RECYCLING CULTURE

Promoting waste management

"Waste is a design flaw."
Kate Krebs, former Director of Sustainable Resources,
The Climate Group

In **Sweden**, an impressive 99% of household waste is recycled, with 50% being burned for energy. Since the 1980s, Swedes have been separating their trash and dropping it in shared containers in apartments or at neighbourhood recycling stations. Citizens can even get cash back for recycling aluminium cans and plastic bottles, resulting in 1.8 billion recycled cans and bottles.

Monetary incentives can be effective both ways. The state of New Hampshire in the **United States** has reduced 800 pounds of municipal wastage annually by introducing a pay-as-you-throw model, where residents must pay one to two dollars per bag of waste. The initiative has halved trash disposal in some towns, encouraging residents to reduce waste and recycle instead.

The **Netherlands**, meanwhile, discourages the purchase of new household and electronic equipment by charging a recycling or removal tax on these items. And the nation's recycling efforts do not stop there – 30% of the human waste in the country is converted into phosphate-rich fertiliser.

"There is no such thing as "away".
When we throw something away it must go somewhere."
Annie Leonard, co-Executive Director of Greenpeace USA

The city of Curitiba in **Brazil** introduced an innovative 'Green Exchange Program' in 1991. It enabled anyone to secure food, bus passes and student notebooks in exchange for recyclables such as paper, cardboard, glass, metal and oil. For every four kilograms of recyclables or two litres of plant or oil handed over, residents could get one kilogram of fresh produce. This helped sell surplus crops while improving nutrition and keeping the environment clean. Additionally, about 62 neighbourhoods swapped 11,000 tons of recyclables for almost a million bus passes. The initiative also provides employment in sorting recyclables to individuals from low-income households. Within a year, 70% of garbage was being recycled. By 2007, the initiative had diverted 45,000 tons of waste from landfill. And Curitiba's paper recycling alone saves 1,200 trees per day.

Encouraging second-hand purchasing

> *"I only feel angry when I see waste.*
> *When I see people throwing away things we could use."*
> *Mother Teresa, nun and founder of*
> *the Order of Missionaries of Charity*

The **Swedes** practice leading minimalistic lifestyles through an intriguing exercise known as *döstädning* or 'death cleaning'. This involves cutting down or limiting your possessions with the understanding that, if left undone, other people will have to tackle all your belongings after your passing.

In 2015, Sweden opened the first mall in the world that sells solely second-hand items, including furniture, computers and electronics, bicycles and books.

The mall makes buying recycled goods convenient and fun by bringing several product categories into a single space. It has a drive-through depot strategically placed next to the city's primary recycling plant, making it easy for citizens to donate goods they no longer need. Items dropped off are sorted by mall staff and stored in one of 11 zones representing the mall's 11 departments. The mall also offers repair and refurbishing services. In 2017, the ReTuna mall sold over USD 1 million worth of items, nearly all of which were donated by the public.

ReTuna mall, Sweden; Source: Wikimedia Commons

Other countries are making similar efforts. **Finland** has opened a chain of large second-hand markets that sell furniture, electronics, books, clothes and much more. And in the **United States**, a 20,000-square-foot centre in Michigan called the 'ReUse Center' specialises in the resale of household, gardening and building materials.

Meanwhile, in **South Africa**, the major clothing retailers donate their excess stock and returned items, which would otherwise be burnt or sent to landfill, to The Clothing Bank. Here, they are de-branded and resold by South African women. This provides financial independence in a nation with the highest rates of unemployment in the world, while benefitting the environment. In 2019, retailers donated over 1.8 million units, valued at cost at USD 8 million. This generated collective profits of about USD 2.4 million for 900 women business owners. Meanwhile, The Appliance Bank empowers South African fathers to repair and resell faulty appliances donated by retailers, once again disrupting the usual cycle of waste disposal.

Fighting waste from the classroom

Some countries are getting kids involved in the quest to manage waste. Before the start of the school year, **Bulgaria** gave children in three major cities the opportunity to earn a free book of their choice – by handing in 5 kilograms of waste paper. Those who handed in an additional 5 kilograms got a free copy of 'Guardians of the Planet' – a book specially printed for the occasion. The event helped collect nearly 300 tons of waste paper while giving over 55,000 children new reading material. **Malta** is also encouraging children to recycle by distributing targeted comic books and board games to all schools. These tell the story of Commander Yellow and General Buzz and their quest to defeat the Garbage Monster through effective waste separation. And students in Berlin, **Germany**, have begun signing climate agreements with their school administrations. These include proposals for an effective waste separation system, comprehensive recycling programmes, a seasonal diet of fruits and vegetables in the cafeteria, and eco-friendly breakfast boxes.

"Pollution is nothing but the resources
we are not harvesting. We allow them to disperse
because we've been ignorant of their value."
R. Buckminster Fuller, American architect,
designer and inventor

Over in the **Ivory Coast**, UNICEF and the Colombian company Conceptos Plasticos are using plastic waste to make modular bricks to build schools. In a country where 1.6 million children do not attend school, partly due to a lack of classrooms, these plastic bricks can help give children an education. The bricks are waterproof and fire-retardant, and the building process doesn't require cement or sand. As a result, classrooms can be built within a month. From 2018 to early 2020, 26 classrooms were built using plastic waste. In fact, UNICEF has now built a plastic brick factory in Ivory Coast. Local women collect the waste plastic for recycling, providing income that can help them to rise above the poverty line.

FIGHTING FOOD WASTE

"Nature provides a free lunch,
but only if we control our appetites."
William Ruckelshaus, first Administrator
of the Environmental Protection Agency

With its strict policies on zero food waste, healthy citizens and sustainable agricultural methods, **France** has topped the Food Sustainability Index multiple times. The year 2015 saw France become the first country to ban edible supermarket food waste. Instead, large supermarkets, mass catering and the high-turnover food industry *must* partner with a charity to donate unsold food. If caught destroying edible food, they could be fined up to 0.1% of their annual turnover.

In France, food waste is first prevented with discounts and awareness. Any remaining food must be donated to charities. If this is not possible, it is used as animal feed or, if that is also not possible, it is used for composting. Only as a last resort is food disposed of.

Other ways in which France leads the fight against food waste are by ensuring that 'best before' dates are included in product codes to streamline logistics, legally requiring commercial caterers to offer a doggy-bag option, and mandating that certain food and mass catering entities publicly declare their commitment to minimising food waste.

Food waste is also tackled at the household level. In 2017, seven-litre recycling containers were distributed to households in Paris along with a guide to recycling food waste. The collected waste is transformed into fertiliser, converted to heat and electricity, or made into biofuel used by buses.

Meanwhile, **South Korea** has gone from a nation that, in 1995, recycled just 2% of its food waste to one that recycles 95%. How did this happen? With smart policy changes. First, it became illegal to dump food in landfill, then it was made mandatory to recycle food waste in biodegradable bags. The cost of the bags (on average USD 6 per household) covers 60% of the cost of running the programme. The bag charges also encourage families to compost waste at home.

The capital city, Seoul, has cut back food waste by 47,000 tonnes in six years. Its success is driven by 6,000 tech-enabled bins that charge residents based on the weight of deposited food waste. The bins, which use scales and RFID technology, have encouraged residents to remove the moisture in food waste to reduce its weight. As food waste is about 80% moisture, this is estimated to have saved USD 8.4 million in collection charges over the six years. Recycled food waste is used as fertiliser or animal feed, while moisture squeezed out of the waste is used to make bio-gas or bio-oil.

In **Denmark**, Princess Marie has helped set up the Wefood supermarket that collects and sells surplus produce, cutting costs by 30-50%. She also works with the Danish food bank FoedevareBanken to provide healthy food options to individuals in need while fighting food waste.

Companies also have a role to play in minimising food waste. Denmark-founded food waste app 'Too Good to Go' connects hungry individuals with excess food at grocery stores, restaurants and bakeries. These items are sold at one-third the retail price, keeping individual portions of food – that can't efficiently be sent to charities and shelters – from becoming waste. Participating on the app allows food businesses to sell more and secure new customers to trial their products. The company has expanded to 15 countries and has 37 million users. Impressively, it has saved over 70 million meals across the world by partnering with more than 87,000 retailers.

In **Germany**, 'Foodsharing Berlin' operates a web-based platform where over 10,000 volunteers coordinate food-sharing. Excess food is collected from supermarkets, bakeries and other businesses and distributed for free to homeless shelters and through publicly available shelves and refrigerators.

Meanwhile, in Rome, **Italy**, food retailers that donate their surplus food enjoy reductions of 25% to even 50% on their municipal waste tax, depending on how much food is donated.

Many countries are also combatting waste throughout the process of food production with vertical farming. This allows crops to be grown indoors, on multiple levels, using hydroponics and technology like LED lights which mimic the sun. These indoor vertical farms use over 90% less water, minimise dependence on environmental conditions, and allow farmland to be converted back into forestland, benefitting the environment. In 2022, **Dubai** opened the world's largest vertical farm – a 30,000-square-foot facility geared to produce over 900 tonnes of leafy greens a year.

5

Gender Equality

A safe and fair world

*"Gender equality is the unfinished business
of the 21st century."*
*Elizabeth Broderick, Australia's
former Sex Discrimination Commissioner*

While no country has entirely eliminated the gender gap, in designing Utopia, there are some countries we can look to that are leading the charge. In fact, a specific region in particular is the trailblazer for gender equality.

For over a decade, **Iceland** has held the number one spot on the Global Gender Gap Index, while other Nordic nations, **Norway**, **Finland** and **Sweden** also rank among the top five most equal countries. What lessons can these nations offer to point us towards a more equal world?

ENABLING EQUAL ECONOMIC OPPORTUNITY

Gender equality in the workplace benefits everyone. And the Nordic countries are making progress. In **Iceland**, 86% of women are in the labour market and 42% of senior officials are women, with 43% female representation on company boards. In **Norway**, women comprise 41% of the C-suite. Meanwhile, **Sweden** ranks fourth in the world for the number of women on corporate boards of directors, with 36% of board members being women. While **Finland** lags behind in board positions for women, its labour force participation gap is 96% closed.

So how do these countries do it? Through practical initiatives that combat discriminatory forces.

Providing paternity leave

When a heterosexual couple has a baby, the woman is often landed with a greater burden of childcare and household responsibilities. As a result, many managers shy away from offering women promotions, seeing them as less available workers. This worsens wage gaps.

> *"Work and care should not sit*
> *at opposite ends of one hard choice."*
> *Elizabeth Broderick, Australia's*
> *former Sex Discrimination Commissioner*

Many countries, led by the Nordic region, have taken measures to correct this imbalance in childcare expectations. In **Norway**, since 2013, both parents must take a minimum of 3.5 months of parental leave following the birth of a child. Both **Icelandic** parents are also entitled to three months of leave each, as well as a bonus three months which they can share. **Finland** is even more generous, offering each parent 160 days (about 5 months) of paid leave. Eligibility for parental leave doesn't depend on employment status, period or type of work. Single parents are eligible for both quotas and free day-care further empowers new parents to return to work. Meanwhile, in **Canada**, parents can share a year of leave at 55% of their salaries.

More and more countries are embracing paternity leave policies. Over the 10 years leading up to 2019, 33 economies from all regions introduced paid paternity leave. It is **Sweden** that provides the most generous parental leave in the world, with new parents eligible to share 480 days – about 16 months – of paid leave after the birth or adoption of a child to be used before the child is eight. Payments are made by the government's Social Insurance Agency.

To offset the notion that any one parent is the primary caregiver, two-parent households can only claim the full benefit if each parent takes 90 days of parental leave.

These initiatives do make a difference. Countries like Sweden report a 7% increase in annual salaries of mothers for every additional month of parental leave taken by fathers. The policies benefit men too – even nine years later, fathers who had taken paternity leave had better relationships with their children.

But many dads don't take the leave they are entitled to. A study of seven countries (Argentina, Brazil, Canada, Japan, Netherlands, the United Kingdom and the United States) found that less than half of fathers took all the leave they were eligible for, with many taking none at all.

Sweden may have an answer. It was the world's first country to replace 'maternity' leave with 'parental' leave back in 1974. Each parent was able to take three months of leave per baby. However, because fathers were able to sign over their days to mothers, 20 years later, women were still taking 90% of leave allocated for fathers. Seeing the need for more robust regulations to overcome status quo bias, Sweden introduced 'pappamånad' (or 'daddy month') in 1995. This was 30 days of leave specifically for dads which couldn't be transferred and would be lost if not taken. This allocation grew to 60 days in 2002 and to 90 days in 2016. The effort made a difference. Out of the total leave days couples could make use of, fathers were taking 30% by 2020.

Denmark, which follows a similar parental leave policy as Sweden, also supports fathers in caring for their young children with more than 25 'Fathers Playrooms' nationwide where fathers can connect with their kids and spend time with other fathers.

"Women are not going to be equal outside the home until men are equal in it."
Gloria Steinem, American journalist and political activist

Mandating equal pay for equal work

The European Union recognises 'Equal Pay Day' as the day when men across the EU have already earned as much as women of the EU will for the entire year. As of 2022, the day is 15 November. Along similar lines, **Austria** recognises its own Equal Pay Day (25 October in 2021) and Equal Pension Day (03 August in 2022) – the day when the average Austrian male pensioner will have earned as much as their female counterpart would earn for the year. The movement of each day (e.g. in 2020, Equal Pay Day in Austria fell on 22 October) marks the nation's current status in terms of wage equality. This makes the gap and progress towards closing it more tangible to all citizens.

Equal pay for work of equal value is an essential part of a just society. But given that no country has entirely eliminated the gender wage gap, where can we look for inspiration?

As at 2021, **Luxembourg** manages an hourly wage gap of just 1.4%. How does it do it?

In 2015, Luxembourg introduced its Ministry of Equality between Women and Men. Here, over 120 public sector equal opportunity representatives strive to ensure workplace equality. Since 2016, with the introduction of the equal pay law, unequal pay has been made an offence and employees can raise concerns and insist on their right to equal pay for work of equal value. Meanwhile, the Ministry's Positive Actions programme certifies companies that show commitment towards equality. Free software is provided for companies to measure wage gaps. The gender equality of the organisation is assessed through an independent survey, and a plan of action prepared in partnership with the Ministry. Companies taking significant action to improve recruitment practices, wages, promotions, training and work-life balance receive the 'Positive Actions' label. These proactive approaches may contribute towards Luxembourg being the wealthiest country per capita with some of the highest living standards in the world.

Iceland, which had closed 84% of its wage gap as of 2021, introduced its equal pay for equal work policy in 2018. This requires all companies with over 25 employees to demonstrate that they pay equally for the same positions and become certified every three years. Since 2020, companies that fail to get certified are subject to a daily fine of USD 500. This matters as research demonstrates that to be effective, certification programmes for equal pay must be strongly enforced. Placing the onus on the employer rather than the employee also boosts effectiveness. Managers follow a two-step system of job evaluation which assigns value to specific job requirements, irrespective of the person occupying the role. Though they acknowledge the process takes time, Icelandic managers appreciate the straightforwardness of the resulting structure and the trust and confidence it produces among employees and new recruits. Employees have also expressed pride in participating in the progressive initiative. And both managers and employees report an improvement in the work environment following the initiative.

In 2018, **Germany** introduced a Wage Transparency Act that empowers employees of companies with over 200 staff members to learn the median pay of colleagues of the opposite gender in the same role or a comparable role. The median is derived from the pay of a minimum of six employees of the opposite sex. This equips staff with the information to challenge pay discrimination.

Other countries are also increasingly embracing wage equality. **Spain** mandates that companies with over 50 employees have gender equality plans including salary audits. And over the decade leading up to 2019, 13 economies — Albania, Belgium, Bolivia, the Comoros, Equatorial Guinea, Liberia, Libya, Mauritius, Montenegro, Serbia, South Africa, Vietnam and Zambia — all introduced laws mandating equal remuneration for work of equal value. Other efforts to combat workplace discrimination include **Norway**'s law that job advertisements cannot specify a gender preference.

ENSURING HEALTH, SAFETY AND SURVIVAL

Combatting gender-based violence

A handful of countries are making serious efforts to crack down on gender-based abuse and violence.

In **Sweden**, preventative, upstream measures are being implemented. In 1955, the country became the first in the world to make sex and gender education compulsory across all schools. Topics such as sexual consent are covered in an eight-week course. Videos, activities and discussions are all accommodated, ensuring that students gain a comprehensive understanding. The priority given to the subject is likely to contribute to the fact that Sweden has among the world's lowest adolescent birth rates – about eight times less than the global average. In **Iceland** too, short films are screened in elementary schools to teach children about violence prevention and consent. Teachers are instructed on how to present the videos, and the school counsellor participates. These programmes help to nurture respect and non-violence in children early in life.

Iceland also strives to respond efficiently when violence does occur. Between 2015 and 2016, the number of reported domestic abuse cases dropped by the police reduced from 94% to just 3% with the introduction of the Keeping the Windows Open project. The project focuses on continuous engagement between abuse victims and support avenues like social workers and the police.

This ongoing interaction is important. Research shows that survivors of abuse return to abusive partners an average of seven times before leaving for good – potentially due to fear of retaliation, financial dependence on the partner, guilt over disrupting the family unit, and myriad other reasons.

The Keeping the Windows Open project revised how domestic abuse cases are handled. Now, when police receive a complaint, a 24/7 operation is put in motion. Social workers join the police to visit the home, serving as specialists in engaging with victims and children. They can also use the knowledge they may have of family history, prior conflicts and cases of abuse. A thorough investigation takes place and suspected abusers may be removed from the home. After a week, there is a follow-up visit and the risk of future violence is assessed. The house is regularly monitored on an ongoing basis thereafter.

Albania assists survivors of gender-based violence with free legal aid services, supporting them in securing information and justice, irrespective of socioeconomic background.

Other countries are running campaigns to promote healthier relationships. **Brazil**'s "Real Men Don't Beat Women" campaign in 2013 featured local male celebrities holding up posters with those five words. The campaign was promoted via popular newspapers and news channels, and the urban metro system in Rio de Janeiro featured it for free. Five key urban transport stations were equipped with over 100 digital information terminals as well as centres providing medical, legal and counselling support for victims of gender-based violence. Similarly, a **Spanish** city ran a campaign leading up to Valentine's Day to tackle unhealthy concepts around relationships, replacing ideas such as 'without you, I am nothing' with messages of self-love and self-affirmation. The goal was to promote self-respect and healthy boundaries over unrealistic expectations and potentially toxic stereotypes.

The COVID-19 pandemic saw increased incidences of domestic abuse as victims of violence were often trapped with perpetrators, and many countries made efforts to respond. **Germany** conducted a "Not safe at home?" campaign across over 26,000 supermarkets to provide information on available support services. Meanwhile, **Ireland**'s "Still here" campaign aimed to convey that the police and courts continued to be available to survivors despite the pandemic. In **France**, 20,000 hotel nights were subsidised for intimate partner violence survivors, while in **Turkey**, 40 properties across 36 provinces were repurposed for survivors. Meanwhile, the **US** city of Chicago, in partnership with Airbnb, made hotel rooms available to house survivors escaping danger.

The **Italian** region of Piedmont uses technology to support its residents, with an app to help them stay safe when navigating the area. An 'SOS' button sends GPS coordinates and a request for help to three pre-registered numbers while a 'Follow me' button allows users to send their geolocation to a contact so their safe travel to a destination can be monitored. It also displays the route (by foot or public transport) and travel time to the nearest shelter. The contact information and locations of the region's anti-violence centres and shelters are also available on the app.

Addressing period poverty

A handful of countries are taking action to alleviate the extra financial burden placed on individuals who are obliged to purchase period products during menstruation. For example, **Canada** has gotten rid of its 5% tax on period products since 2016.

But it was **Kenya** that was the first country in the world to get rid of the 'tampon tax' (the taxes placed on period products) and begin making pads freely available in public schools in 2018. Free pads were then distributed in rural and underserved communities, a measure that educators report has boosted school attendance. **Scotland** also makes period products freely available at schools, pharmacies, community centres and youth clubs. In 2017, it was the first to make sanitary products freely available in schools, and in 2020, it became the first to make tampons and pads freely available to anyone in need of them. In 2021, **New Zealand** also ensured that all schools in the country provide tampons and pads free of charge to boost school attendance and tackle period poverty. Meanwhile, free period products are also provided in the schools of various states across Australia, Canada and the United States.

Other countries provide menstrual leave to allow those suffering from debilitating menstrual cramps to take a day or more off work to manage the pain. **Japan** has done so for over 70 years, although few people actually claim the unpaid leave due to stigma. In **South Korea**, disallowing period leave can lead employers to face jail time, and women should be compensated for unused period leave. **Zambia** offers one day of period leave per month, and **Taiwan** three, while more and more provinces and businesses in **India** and **China** are introducing various period leave policies. In 2022, **Spain** became the first country in Europe to draft legislation offering three to five days of period leave.

While some argue that menstrual leave policies can encourage discrimination against employing women, others feel that those who experience dysmenorrhea (severe menstrual cramps) should have the right to relief.

Ensuring reproductive rights

When surveys showed that fewer women under 25 were using contraception as they couldn't afford it, **France** took action, making birth control free to all women under 25 from the start of 2021. The initiative protects the rights of about three million women and includes a range of contraceptive options including the pill, IUDs, contraceptive patches, and more. The **United Kingdom**'s National Health Service also makes contraception available for free at pharmacies and clinics, ensuring that income levels do not affect family planning efforts.

According to the World Health Organisation (WHO), 61% of all unintended pregnancies end in induced abortion. The WHO reports that limiting access to abortions doesn't actually lower the number that take place, but instead influences whether abortions are performed safely. In countries where abortion laws are restrictive, significantly more unsafe abortions take place.

Global estimates suggest that about 45% of induced abortions are unsafe, and about one-third occur by persons without training and using dangerous, invasive methods. Every year, 5-13% of maternal deaths occur due to unsafe abortion.

What do laws on abortion look like around the world?

- As of 2022, 36% of women live in the 72 countries that allow abortion on request, with varying gestational limits, 12 weeks being the most common. These countries include Australia, Canada, Iceland, Norway, South Africa, Sweden, Thailand, Vietnam, and many more.

- 23% of women live in countries that permit abortions with consideration of a woman's social or economic circumstances. These countries include Ethiopia, Finland, India, Japan, Taiwan, and Zambia.
- 14% of women live in countries that permit abortion on health grounds. These countries include Bolivia, Ecuador, Israel, Jordan, Pakistan, Peru, Poland, Malaysia, Saudi Arabia, and about half of the African nations.
- 22% of women live in 42 countries that allow abortion only when it is necessary to save the woman's life. These countries include Afghanistan, Brazil, Chile, Indonesia, Iran, Mexico, Somalia, Sri Lanka, Syria and Uganda.
- And 5% of women live in the 24 countries that prohibit abortions under any circumstance, including when a woman's life is at risk. These include Egypt, Haiti, Honduras, Iraq, Madagascar, Philippines and Sierra Leone.

Iceland presently has one of Europe's most permissive abortion laws, enabling abortion on request up to 22 weeks at the sole discretion of the pregnant adult or minor. Yet 94% of abortions in Iceland occur before the 12th week of pregnancy.

97% of unsafe abortions occur in developing countries, violating women's and girls' right to life and to the highest possible standard of physical and mental health. Women and girls facing unsafe abortions can experience physical health risks such as haemorrhage, infection, perforation of the uterus, damage to the genital tract and internal organs, etc. There are economic consequences too, disproportionately affecting the developing world. Developing countries lose over USD 920 million annually in household income as a result of long-term disability due to unsafe abortions. On top of this, unsafe abortions are estimated to cost developing countries' health systems over USD 550 million annually for post-abortion treatments.

Tackling postpartum depression

> *"The health of a mother and child is a more telling measure of a nation's state than economic indicators."*
> Harjit Gill, CEO of APACMed

Postpartum depression is experienced by one in five women. Countries with the lowest rates include **Singapore** (3%), **Nepal** (7%), the **Netherlands** (8%), and **Switzerland** (11%). A study of over 295,000 women worldwide found that economic status and healthcare quality explain 74% of the difference in postpartum depression levels across countries. Lack of assistance provided to mothers who work full-time also worsens the problem.

In **Singapore**, public healthcare institutions provide mental health support to pregnant mothers as part of routine obstetrics care. Women are screened for depression and severe anxiety during pregnancy as well as 2-8 weeks after the baby's birth, and can be referred to a dedicated psychiatry clinic in the Singapore General Hospital. A team comprising a case manager, psychiatrist, occupational therapist and psychologist provide support to women experiencing postpartum depression.

Singapore is also experimenting with providing mobile-based peer support from trained lay volunteers who have previously experienced postpartum depression. Results look positive, with a reported 20% drop in the risk of developing postpartum depression.

According to UNICEF, home visits from nurses who assess the mother's condition and provide qualified psychosocial support also has documented success in reducing postpartum depression. Such efforts offer helpful insight into how to prioritise mothers' mental health.

Providing gender-sensitive medical care

The **Austrian** state of Carinthia is training its doctors on gender-sensitive medical care, recognising that symptoms often present differently in female and male bodies. One example is heart attacks – while for men, the most common symptom is chest pain, this is rare among women, who are more likely to experience nausea, vomiting, and jaw and back pain. The result is that women sometimes receive treatment too late. Similarly, while aspirin can lower the risk of heart disease among men, it can have the opposite effect among women. Ensuring that the medical system accounts for such differences can save lives.

Protecting sex worker rights

Around the world, tens of millions of women work in the sex industry, in addition to millions of men and non-binary individuals. Many in the industry see no other practical avenue out of financial hardship. The International Labour Organisation (ILO) estimates that sex workers support between five and eight other people with their earnings.

Criminalising sex work gives sex workers little choice but to accept working conditions that are often exploitative. In 2003, **New Zealand** decriminalised sex work and protected sex workers via employment and human rights laws. Contrary to concerns, the industry size did not grow following the change. Instead, a study by the Christchurch School of Medicine found that over 90% of sex workers believed the law gave them legal and health and safety rights. 64% found it easier to refuse clients and 57% reported improved attitudes of the police towards them.

The New Zealand scenario suggests that decriminalisation can empower sex workers to prosecute those who violate their rights and to report cases of trafficking and underage prostitution without fear of persecution by authorities. It also enables better regulation of the industry, for example, with zoning rules, improved security, mandatory contraception use and regular medical check-ups.

Additionally, taxation of the industry enables governments to use the funds to pay for programmes that can help those who would like to find a path out of sex work to do so.

PROVIDING POLITICAL EMPOWERMENT

Acting collectively for gender equality

Iceland has greater gender equality across parliament, ministries and heads of state than any other nation – 75% as of 2021. The country performs about 10% better than second-ranked Norway and about four times better than the global average. How has Iceland reached this point?

1975 was declared by the United Nations as a 'Women's Year'. To mark the occasion while making a statement, the Icelandic feminist movement the 'Red Stockings' suggested a strike. Other feminist organisations agreed, but to secure widespread support and avoid participants facing disciplinary action from employers, the strike was called a 'day off'.

90% of women in Iceland participated, and 24th October 1975 saw 25,000 women band together as a unified force, ceasing their professional and domestic roles to take to the streets. Icelandic society immediately felt their absence – housekeeping, cooking and childcare were interrupted, shops, factories and theatres could not open, dads took children to work as most schools and nurseries were closed, flights were grounded, telephone exchanges went unanswered, newspapers could not print, and some radio broadcasts had to shut down. The indispensability of women was clear as the streets filled with protest signs and the sounds of cheering, whistling, and banging pots.

Within five years, president Vigdís Finnbogadóttir had become the first democratically elected female president in the world. And Iceland's tradition continues over 45 years later, with the Women's Day Off having taken place five more times – with no signs of stopping. 2016 saw women in Iceland ceasing work at exactly 2:38 pm – the time when the wage gap indicates that women technically stop being paid while men continue to be paid.

Interest in the subject of gender is high throughout the nation – as of 2016, a whopping one-third of all Icelandic women were part of a closed Facebook group to discuss gender-related matters. The group is ironically named 'Beauty Tips'.

Boosting visibility of female political leaders

Iceland had the first democratically elected female president in the world in the 1980s. A single mother, Vigdís Finnbogadóttir was popular and respected, leading her to secure three subsequent re-elections. Indeed, Iceland has had a female president for 22 of the 50 years leading up to 2020. Jóhanna Sigurðardóttir became the country's first female prime minister in 2009, breaking another record for Iceland as the world's first openly gay head of state.

In 1908, the first women elected to municipal government, and those elected in 1922 to parliament, were represented by women's lists rather than traditional political parties. When a new political party – The

Women's Alliance – was set up in 1982, there was a jump in female political participation and the 1983 election saw a trifold increase in women MPs, from five to 15 out of 60. The Women's Alliance put women's concerns on the agenda and led to the establishment of the first emergency reception centre for victims of sexual violence.

Iceland does not have legal quotas on women's parliamentary representation, though some parties do insist that a minimum number of candidates must be women. Out of the established political parties, only one does not have any gender representation rules such as a 'zipper system' (which alternates the names of men and women to ensure women are not at the bottom of the list) when placing men and women on candidate lists. As of 2021, 30 out of 63 seats in parliament (48%) are occupied by women.

And while other countries frown on public breastfeeding, it is considered completely normal in Iceland. The best example is perhaps when a Member of Parliament breastfed her baby during parliament in 2016.

Another top-ranking country for gender equality, **Finland** was the first country to award women full political rights in 1906. It also boasts the world's youngest female prime minister, Sanna Marin (34 years when elected in 2019). Indeed, Finland's minister of education, minister of finance and interior minister were all women under the age of 35 when appointed to their posts.

Finland does not have statutory gender quotas, yet had a 47% share of women in parliament in 2020. Since 1987, Finnish women have been more active as voters compared to men. And studies reveal that women increasingly vote for female candidates – in the 1991 parliamentary election, 58% of women voted for women, and the percentage doing so has since remained over 50%. This suggests that once a threshold level of normalisation of female leadership has been achieved, the need for quotas reduces as societies collectively embrace female leadership.

In 2020, the representation of women in **Sweden**'s parliament was 47%, with 54% of ministerial positions held by women. While Sweden doesn't have legislated quotas for female representation, political parties have adopted voluntary quotas over the years.

Research from the Inter-Parliamentary Union (IPU) shows that the type of electoral system a country has in place influences the level of representation of women in parliaments, with the share of elected women notably higher in proportional and mixed systems as compared with majoritarian systems. Majoritarian systems award the majority of seats in parliament to parties and candidates who secure the largest portion of votes, even if the actual portion of votes secured is below 50%. Proportional systems, on the other hand, allocate seats based on the share of votes each party secures, with seats assigned to candidates based on the party's electoral list. Mixed systems, meanwhile, combine features from both majoritarian and proportional systems. Iceland, Finland and Sweden all follow proportional electoral systems.

Introducing quotas for equal representation

Countries with more women in leadership enjoy economic and social benefits. The presence and support of female leaders encourage more women to work and occupy leadership roles. 75% of women across all Nordic countries are employed, resulting in lower income inequality compared with countries like the United States and the United Kingdom where a smaller proportion of women are employed. Additionally, when a country has more women in power, it is more likely to introduce legal policies that boost equality. Nations with more female legislators also saw some of the most effective national responses to COVID-19.

In order to reap such rewards, many countries make use of gender quotas to ensure representation. **Norway**, for example, legislates for 40% female representation in parliament and on corporate boards. In 2021, Norway had a majority female parliament, with 10 of 19 ministerial posts being held by women. And in 2018, women held the posts of prime minister, minister of finance and minister of foreign affairs.

Meanwhile, **Spain** has seen a growth in the share of women in parliament since enacting a law in 2007 requiring at least 40% female representation on party election lists. In 2019, the country boasted 65% women ministers and 47% women parliamentarians.

But the country that leads the way in female parliamentary representation is **Rwanda**, which has held the top spot every year for over a decade. As of 2022, 61% of its members of parliament are women. Following the genocide, the 2013 Constitution mandates at least 30% female representation in parliament. Indeed, by law, at least 30% of posts in *all* decision-making bodies must be held by women.

Prioritising equality through policy

In the 1960s, East **Germany** introduced policy changes to realise legal equality between men and women and to promote women's economic participation. To support women's active professional and social involvement, kindergartens were set up and childcare facilities provided in firms, substantial maternity leave was introduced and paid leave was provided for handling domestic work. Publications encouraged women's workforce participation with depictions of women working as journalists, professors, brigadiers and factory workers. The 70s and 80s then saw the introduction of the "mothers' policy" (Mutti-Politik) which provided more flexible working hours, holidays and paid leaves. It also reserved space for women in jobs and universities, and enabled family planning with the 'desired child pill' (Wunschkindpill), provided free of charge. As a result of these efforts, women's participation in the East German workforce in 1990 was 89%, not far behind men's participation rate of 92%.

Sweden is the first country in the world to describe itself as a 'feminist government' prioritising gender equality when making decisions and allocating resources. Its parental leave policy, the most generous in the world, is among the efforts that have helped Sweden close more than 80% of its gender gap. In 2014, Sweden became the first in the world to introduce a 'feminist foreign policy', whereby gender equality is considered in all foreign policy efforts.

Another Nordic country, **Norway** was the world's first nation to have a gender equality ombud, whom any person can contact for guidance on laws and matters regarding gender equality. Meanwhile, **Finland** has a dedicated Act on Equality between Women and Men to prioritise equality legislation. And **Rwanda**'s Gender Monitoring Office tracks whether public programmes comply with the country's gender equality goals. All these efforts serve to prioritise gender equality on the national agenda, allowing countries to reap the social and economic rewards.

ACCELERATING CULTURAL CHANGE

Calling out media stereotypes

The media consumed by the public has the power to shape culture, convey social expectations and imply an individual's place in society. Therefore, the **United Kingdom** has banned advertising that perpetuates stereotypes about gender roles. Advertisements such as those featuring men displaying incompetence in parenting and women appearing passive alongside adventurous males have been removed from screens. The effort strives to challenge the media's capacity to limit how men and women view themselves.

Educating youth on equality

Education can be a powerful tool to break down societal stereotypes. In **Iceland**, the law requires that gender equality is taught at school. A gender studies subject is compulsorily on the curriculum of over 80% of the country's high schools. It aims to make students aware of discrimination and critically analyse all aspects of society. The subject tackles topics such as violence, gendered jokes, prostitution, pornography, music videos, workplaces and politics.

Additionally, many Icelandic nurseries and primary schools practice the 'Hjalli method'. This method separates boys and girls at the youngest ages to protect them from inevitable gender comparisons and support them as they develop the traits considered typical of the opposite gender. The activities, toys, educational facilities and uniforms are all unisex but the programme actively strives to encourage girls to take up space and use their voices, while encouraging boys to express compassion and verbalise emotions. In doing so, it combats the cultural stereotypes girls and boys inevitably come up against – and research shows it works in developing youth with a stronger understanding of equality.

"We've begun to raise daughters more like sons... but few have the courage to raise our sons more like our daughters."
Gloria Steinem, American journalist and political activist

Teacher training matters too. In **Croatia**, primary school teachers are trained to recognise their own unconscious gender biases and understand how stereotyping words and beliefs can have a long-term impact on children's educational, career and life choices. Meanwhile, **Finland**'s Ministry of Culture and Education supported the distribution of free copies of Chimamanda Ngozi Adichie's book *We Should All Be Feminists* to all ninth-grade students in 2017. The short book provides an introduction to key gender equality issues through stories from the author's life.

Introducing equality in religion

Icelandic culture is also striving to introduce gender equality in religion. For example, a priest at one of the country's largest church congregations refers to God in gender-neutral terms when she speaks, sometimes replacing 'He' with 'She' or 'It'. This first occurred in 1974, when Iceland's first female priest referred to God as 'She'.

6

Public Spaces

The ideal architecture for living

"In the utopia, architecture would more fairly be interpreted as a branch of mental health, with a crucial role to play in public contentment. And bad design would – at last – be interpreted as the crime it is to the health of the collective spirit."
Alain de Botton, author of The Architecture of Happiness

It shouldn't surprise anyone that Utopia would be a beautiful place to live in. A visual paradise, with every turn offering a treat for the eyes. It would support Utopian lifestyles, promoting function as well as aesthetic appreciation. But what approaches can we take to make such a living space a reality?

According to Alain de Botton, author of *The Architecture of Happiness* and honorary fellow of the Royal Institute of British Architects, if we fully appreciated the capacity of ugly architecture to 'sap our spirits and give assistance to our worst selves', we would legislate against it.

As tourist statistics reveal, there are many beautiful cities around the world. And introducing some of their features could make other cities beautiful too. Let's explore some of the world's most delightful destinations – and consider how to replicate their success.

DESIGNING BEAUTIFUL CITIES

Embracing the arts

"If you have but two coins, use one for bread to feed the body and the other for hyacinths to feed the soul."
Persian proverb

With a strong connection to wellbeing, art contributes to a beautiful environment. Whether painting, sculpture, film or music, making space for the arts with venues, galleries and installations can help cultivate a wholesome and happy living space.

Appreciating the value of art, the mayor of Cincinnati, Ohio in the **United States** made a 'Mural Proclamation' to have at least one large streetside wall painting brightening up each of the city's neighbourhoods. The city now has over 145 murals.

Similarly, the city of Richmond in Virginia set up the Richmond Mural Program with the aim of creating 100 murals on city walls. But it's Philadelphia that is called the 'mural capital of the world' with over 4,000 murals making up the world's largest outdoor art gallery. Guided tours of the murals are offered by foot, segway, trolley and train.

Other American cities renowned for street art are Detroit in Michigan, home to one of the world's largest international mural festivals, and Denver in Colorado, which hosts the Denver Chalk Art Festival every summer.

Woman walks past a mural; Source: Max Pixel

The **Irish** town of Drogheda uses murals to keep its local mythology alive, with streetside artwork that celebrates stories from its culture and heritage. What's more, the murals aren't just beautiful – they also discourage rogue artists from vandalising city walls. In 2010, the **Portuguese** capital, Lisbon, launched the Crono Project, encouraging artists to set their imaginations to work on the deteriorating façades of old buildings. This initiative transformed former eyesores into visual feasts. The city even boasts an urban art park which offers graffiti artists dedicated walls for painting, alongside space for skating and the performing arts.

Meanwhile, **Denmark**'s city of Varde boasts 111 sculptures which can be toured with a virtual or physical guide describing the history of each piece.

In **Lithuania**, public bus stops form the venue for the city's 'largest art gallery'. Instead of the typical advertising, the stops feature paintings by local artists. The project provides commuters with the chance to enjoy an outdoor exhibition while giving visibility to artists, as well as the opportunity for them to sell their works.

British artist Luke Jerram and his team have taken a different approach to add creativity and music to public spaces. They have installed over 2,000 pianos in the parks, streets, markets and train stations of more than 65 cities, from New York to Tokyo. Each piano bears the words 'Play Me, I'm Yours' and local artists and communities have painted and decorated them. Luke's idea was to catalyse conversation and connection in public spaces – and the project has done just that, even leading to marriages between individuals who met around the pianos!

Boy plays a public piano; Source: Choo Yut Shing, Flickr

Regulating building scale

Joseph Campbell said, "If you want to see what a society really believes in, look at what the biggest buildings on the horizon are dedicated to". Accordingly, Alain de Botton advises that massive corporations should not be allowed free rein to dominate the skyline with skyscrapers and ugly behemoths of buildings.

In 1971, in the city of Boulder, Colorado in the **United States**, Ruth Wright, a citizen activist, led a successful campaign to prevent the city council from allowing buildings as high as 14 stories. Her ballot measure effectively limited building heights to five stories, ensuring that the residents of Boulder would continue to enjoy lush mountain views. Today, Wright is nearly 90 years old, and still actively engaged in preserving the character of her community.

"Had I lost, Boulder would be a forest of high-rises crisscrossed by traffic-jammed streets."
Ruth Wright, 88-year-old citizen activist
from Boulder, Colorado

According to de Botton, beautiful and wholesome cities are the result of strict and ambitious regulations. He stresses that city regulation should ensure that the maximum height of any city block is five stories high, as can be seen in the most attractive parts of Berlin, Amsterdam, London, and Paris.

The recipe for an attractive city, he insists, is simple: densely built five-storey buildings with large windows, contemporary forms and natural materials, and streets lively with pedestrian activity. In the **United Kingdom**, Edinburgh's New Town, for example, presented exacting legislation detailing heights for buildings, quality of finish, the width of pavements, and the character of the skyline.

Balancing order with variety

Apart from regulation of building scale, de Botton recommends introducing order into the planning of cities, while allowing for variety within the prescribed pattern. Order, symmetry and repetition provide a pleasing sense of balance and structure. But uniqueness within the pattern is also desirable as too much order can feel rigid and boring.

Governments have the opportunity to regulate the pattern of buildings while giving building owners freedom of interpretation in style. De Botton points to the Main Square in Telč in the **Czech Republic** and to Javaeiland in **Amsterdam** for examples of beautiful sites where every house is the same width and height but allowed to freely vary its form and colour. The result is a beautiful balance between methodical and interesting.

Main Square in Telč, Czech Republic; Source: Wikimedia Commons

Adding local flavour

Master architect Liu Thai Ker, who was responsible for the transformation of **Singapore**, stresses that every locality's design should be influenced by its climate and customs, its architectural heritage and its density. As an example, he describes how many countries which experience strong sunlight, such as those in Asia, tend to shy away from bold colours on buildings, as the sun quickly fades bright colours.

This concept of designing to suit the local environment and culture is favoured by de Botton as well, who advocates that cities should not look identical across the world, but have their own character, and make use of distinctive local materials and forms.

Cultivating compactness and intimacy

De Botton also advocates for the design of cities where citizens can see the activity of daily life unfolding. This adds interest to the environment and a sense of connection to fellow beings. To help make this a reality, he recommends that cities feature plenty of squares – recreational public spaces for people to come together. These, he says, should be intimate spaces, within 30 meters in diameter, allowing someone to see the face of a person on the opposite side.

The much-celebrated Piazza di Santa Maria in **Rome** provides an example of a cosy city square. Even Walt Disney created the entrance of Disneyland to be a replication of the Main Street and town square from history. And the people of San Luis Obispo designed the Mission Plaza to help residents foster social connections and enjoy the arts. Such spaces give pedestrians a pleasant environment to connect and engage.

Crown Fountain, Chicago, USA; Source: Cultivar413, Flickr

De Botton argues that while we typically try to claim as much space for ourselves as possible, having other human beings in proximity uplifts the human spirit. According to de Botton, many of the most loved cities feature lots of cosy little back streets and small lanes. There's an element of enigma and intimacy to these streets which people adore. He describes how, at Cartagena, in **Colombia**, the balconies nearly touch across the street. This allows homeowners more chances to connect with their neighbours and to feel a little less lonely. There's also an environmental benefit to creating dense cities. As de Botton says, "A compact city like Barcelona swallows a fraction of the energy of a sprawling one like Phoenix."

Making technology beautiful

De Botton describes how creative architecture can make visual masterpieces of the technology and functional tools that we usually hide away. As an example, he describes how upset we'd be to hear of a large pipeline being constructed across a river, yet tourists gleefully purchase trips to see the Roman Pont du Gard in Southern **France**, a giant bridge-aqueduct that has been built for both functionality *and* beauty.

For a simple example, we can take the case of a brightly painted bench in the city of Lille, **France**. The colourful bench is in fact a rainwater storage facility, able to collect rainwater through its covering and store it for later use in irrigating plants. This art of making technology pleasing to the eye and spirit can go a long way towards creating a beautiful living environment.

Another example is the CopenHill in **Denmark**, the world's cleanest waste-to-energy power plant that converts Copenhagen's waste into heat and energy, heating about 99% of the city's buildings. Taking advantage of the scale of the power plant, architects have repurposed the roof of the building into an artificial ski slope and introduced the world's tallest climbing wall, as well as challenging hiking trails along the building's slope. As a result, a power plant that serves 680,000 people is now a recreational hotspot.

GREENING COMMUNITY SPACES

Cultivating green cities

Apart from cooling cities and lowering pollution levels, green spaces also provide a treat to the eyes and boost physical and mental health. One **Polish** city, Warsaw, even decided to calculate the monetary value of its trees in improving air quality and citizens' health. Special software was used to measure biophysical indicators and identify oxygen produced, carbon dioxide absorbed and air purification achieved. The answer was found to be, impressively, around USD 37.5 million.

*"Even if I knew that tomorrow the world would go to pieces,
I would still plant my apple tree."*
Martin Luther King Jr., civil rights activist

California's San Luis Obispo in the **United States** gives priority to green spaces, with a rigorous greenbelt plan and regulations that limit housing growth to 1% annually. To reduce suburban sprawl, green spaces close to the town are bought by a natural resources manager who actively raises funds to do so. Beautiful spaces such as parks, wildlife preserves, and trails for hiking and mountain biking are plainly visible to enjoy and to invite residents to get active.

In 1967, **Singapore**'s renowned prime minister Lee Kuan Yew announced his vision of building Singapore into a 'garden city' of tree-lined boulevards and lush greenery. Within three years, over 55,000 trees were planted. An annual tree planting day was introduced to keep the momentum. Public and private entities were also required to make space for greenery. These efforts were successful – between 1974 and 2014, the number of new trees exploded from about 160,000 to 1.4 million. Master architect Liu Thai Ker, credited for the city's transformation, describes his use of a 'chessboard approach' to make even high-density spaces beautiful by alternating buildings with green spaces. **Brazil**'s Curitiba city similarly planted more than 1.5 million trees since the 1970s and set up 28 public parks. With $52m^2$ of green space per resident, Curitiba is one of the world's greenest cities.

Other sites are taking alternative approaches to greening cities – in San Francisco, **USA** and Córdoba, **Spain**, for example, bylaws have been passed requiring that every building with rooftop space of at least 400 square metres must grow a green roof. In Salzburg, **Austria**, a mathematical formula has been introduced for calculating how much green space a building should accommodate with green roofs, green façades and greenery around the structure. A spreadsheet algorithm calculates the requirement based on floor area, façade area and roof area, and the results should be submitted alongside the building plan when applying for a permit.

Meanwhile, **Denmark** has invited all its municipalities to compete for the title of 'Denmark's Wildest Municipality' by introducing green projects that would boost biodiversity. In its bid for the title, the municipality of Horsens has set aside 50,000 square metres for plants and insects and distributed free flower seeds for associations to create meadows.

Growing new forests

> *"Away, away, from men and towns,*
> *To the wildwood and the downs,*
> *To the silent wilderness,*
> *Where the soul need not repress its music."*
> *Percy Bysshe Shelley, English poet*

Some cities are even growing new forests for recreation, biodiversity and better air quality. In **Croatia**, drones are being used to eject seed bombs across large areas of land in the world's first afforestation project that uses drone technology. Meanwhile, in Sofia, **Bulgaria**, a forest of 100,000 trees has been planted by volunteers from the community, private companies and government offices. It is now being followed by another forest of 86,000 trees. Similarly, the Piedmont region of **Italy** is inviting citizens, farms, associations and companies to support it in building a shared forest by contributing about USD 20 to plant and maintain a tree. The goal is to eventually have as many trees as residents in the area – 1.5 million.

The **Romanian** city of Iași has also invited its citizens to adopt a newly planted neighbourhood tree. Adoptive parents will receive a certificate and be able to name the tree, which will show up on a digital map of the city. They will then take care of the tree as it grows and report any problems to the local authorities.

Over in the **Slovak** city of Banská Bystrica, linden trees have been planted as living memorials of those who lost their lives due to the COVID-19 pandemic. These trees were specially selected as they live for around 100 years, grow to a height of 30 metres, are known for their medicinal properties and have heart-shaped leaves.

Caring for recreational spaces

For about five years, the **Danish** municipality of Randers has been giving community associations the chance to earn cash for collecting rubbish in its forests and along its nature trails. Garbage bags, gloves, vests and other equipment are provided and participants can earn more for cleaning longer and more difficult routes.

> *"To me, a lush carpet of pine needles or spongy grass*
> *is more welcome than the most luxurious Persian rug."*
> *Helen Keller, American author and disability rights advocate*

Meanwhile, in the **Netherlands**, citizens are invited to enjoy the sport of stand-up paddle boarding along the historic Hague canals for free – provided they also pick up any trash they find along the route. Each year, 120 tons of waste is removed, mainly blown by the wind from the streets into the water.

The city of Songdo in **South Korea** has adopted a unique method for eliminating rubbish from its streets. Instead of the typical garbage collection system, a network of pneumatic pipes directly sends waste from homes to underground waste processing facilities. As a result, garbage and garbage trucks are virtually unseen!

FAVOURING THE PEDESTRIAN

Prioritising road safety

Over a million people die each year in road-related accidents, costing the majority of countries about 3% of their gross domestic product. In fact, road-related incidents are the biggest threat to the lives of people between 5 to 29 years. So how can we create an environment that is safer and healthier?

Sweden is taking street safety seriously, introducing an array of measures that have halved the number of traffic deaths. This includes fewer intersections, additional roundabouts and pedestrian bridges, separations between bicycles and vehicles, stricter policing of drunk driving, and restrictions on vehicles turning where people cross the road. The country's goal is to bring road-related deaths to zero.

Redesigning public spaces

But many countries and cities are going further – creating public spaces where getting around on foot, by bike or using public transport is easier than travelling by car. This has the added benefit of improving citizen wellbeing. For example, the pedestrian-friendly design in New York City's Times Square actually started as an experiment with temporary markings. The change was so enthusiastically embraced, it was made permanent.

The **Spanish** city of Pontevedra has turned the usual hierarchy of mobility priorities on its head. The city is designed to favour pedestrians and wheelchair users first and foremost, then bicycles, then public transport, and finally private vehicles. In the words of the mayor: "Our attitude is 'park and walk'. Owning a car doesn't come with the right to park it and 'privatise' what is actually public space." The city renovated public spaces and introduced 40 km of footpaths, new street furniture and lighting. It reduced the number of vehicles from 52,000 in 1997 to 17,000 today. Now, the majority of travel happens on foot and over 80% of children walk to school. Traffic management schemes have been put in place and the average vehicle speed is only 25 kilometres per hour. Road deaths have dropped to zero. The city has also seen a nearly 70% reduction in carbon emissions, and an increase in jobs and economic activity.

Encouraging soft mobility

Germany's city of Heidelberg has been redesigned to discourage car use, with a system of bicycle superhighways and hydrogen-powered buses. Vehicle owners who give up their cars are incentivised with one year of free public transport. Meanwhile, in Berlin, where residents already prefer to travel by foot over any other option, a city committee has been established dedicated to pedestrians and furthering their mobility and safety. The city is also developing a 38 km cycling expressway that will pass through six city districts.

The **Netherlands** has also invested in infrastructure to support cyclists, including over 30,000 km of bike lanes, often protected with barriers, and some cyclist-only by-lanes. Cycling lessons are common in schools and drivers must keep to low speeds when sharing road space with cyclists. The investment has paid off – in cities such as Amsterdam, more than two-thirds of travel happens by bike or on foot. San Luis Obispo in the **United States** has similarly introduced wide sidewalks and bike lanes and given cyclists the right-of-way, while new buildings must have bike lockers and shower facilities. The **Swedish** city of Karlstad is even awarding and recognising the most 'bicycle-friendly workplaces'. Also in Sweden, the town of Enköping is getting residents involved in taking care of its cycling paths – with a mobile game. The game allows users to collect virtual fruits while they cycle by placing their mobile phone in a phone holder to film the paths they travel over. The virtual fruits can then be exchanged for real cash and the town uses the information gained for path repair and maintenance.

Over 1,000 cities worldwide now offer bicycle-sharing systems for mechanical and electric bikes, including Barcelona, Dubai, Montreal, New York and Paris. These programmes make public bicycles visibly available throughout the city for residents to rent. In some instances, bikes can be rented from one docking station and returned at another one elsewhere, while in others, dockless bikes can be located, rented and unlocked using a mobile app.

Woman uses a public bike sharing system; Source: Pexels

Other cities are investing in teaching soft mobility skills to youth. **Denmark**'s municipality of Aalborg has teamed up with second-hand shops to offer kindergarteners restored bicycles for free, donated by citizens for recycling. In Vienna, **Austria**, children in grades three and four are given free cycling lessons. And in the city of Tallinn in **Estonia**, a 'cycling school' has been set up to teach traffic rules and grant bicycle licenses to children aged 10 to 15. Those who secure licenses are granted about USD 100 towards buying a bicycle. Meanwhile, in the **Finnish** city of Vallensbæk, all children and adults are invited to join bicycle rides around the municipality, with the mayor as their guide.

Some cities are introducing unique ways of reclaiming the streets from vehicles. For example, in Dortmund, **Germany**, a group of neighbours can petition the local youth welfare office to close their streets off to traffic, giving residents the chance to play football or badminton, throw a block party, and get to know their neighbours. Meanwhile, the **Croatian** city of Kaštela is helping its residents stay outdoors for longer. Its streets feature smart benches that use clean solar energy to provide free device charging, enabling citizens to work, study and relax outdoors.

SUPPORTING HEALTHY LIVING

The Californian city of San Luis Obispo in the **United States** was named by National Geographic's Dan Buettner as the Happiest City in the United States. It boasts a vibrant downtown, green spaces, community areas, a farmers' market, a flourishing arts scene, and less traffic and pollution. All of this was achieved through designing an environment where it's easy to do what's healthy – walking, cycling, eating vegetables and spending time in nature – and harder to do what's unhealthy, such as eating fast food and smoking. What can other locales do to recreate such a healthy, thriving space?

Minimising marketing

"Signs beget more signs." This was the rallying cry of San Luis Obispo mayor Ken Schwartz and graphic artist Pierre Rademaker, who pointed out that the presence of large, bright, blinking signs outside one establishment encourages competing businesses to introduce yet more prominent signage to compete for customer attention. By regulating the scale and nature of signage, San Luis Obispo has kept its city beautiful with simple, small and tasteful signage. As a side effect, residents face less temptation to make needless purchases. This leads to healthier decision-making.

Research validates that policies which scale back fast food signage effectively reduce fast food consumption, improving citizen health while minimising the burden on the healthcare system. Indeed, Michael Pollan, author of *In Defense of Food*, has made the popular health recommendation, "Don't buy any food you've ever seen advertised." In spaces without advertisements, it's easy to see how people will naturally lead healthier lives.

In the capital of **Slovakia**, Bratislava, strict regulations have been introduced on the placement and size of advertising structures – advertising cannot be placed in green spaces, and billboards cannot exceed specified sizes nor obstruct views of city skylines and landmarks. The city has instead decorated its streets with good news – city signage depicts charmingly illustrated stories of good things that happened around the globe during 2021, from children enjoying classes by the beach to people playing music from their balconies. The stories are excerpts from a book called 'The Year of Good News' by Slovak author Martin Smatana.

Eliminating drive-through restaurants

San Luis Obispo has banned drive-through restaurants. While its original goal was to lessen the culture of car use, a positive side-effect has been a reduction of obesity and its associated healthcare costs. As Winston Churchill said, "We shape our buildings: thereafter they shape us." By eliminating the convenience of an unhealthy choice, the town is making being healthy the most convenient option.

Introducing anti-substance use policies

It's lonely to be a smoker in San Luis Obispo. In an effort to de-normalise smoking and promote residents' health, the city has stringent bans on smoking in workplaces, parks, bars, and in front of offices. Not seeing others smoking helps individuals make healthier choices for themselves.

In Boston in the **United States**, a gym called The Phoenix has a unique approach to fighting substance abuse. Its only price of membership is 48 hours of sobriety. The free gym helps individuals struggling with addiction to leverage the power of exercise in their route to recovery. As of 2021, The Phoenix has spread to 53 cities across the United States with nearly 60,000 members.

Establishing community spaces

Community spaces offer the chance for healthy socialising – a key contributor to both wellbeing and lifespan. In Horsens, **Denmark**, a youth cultural hub has been set up to promote music, art and local culture. It includes a café where young people can meet to chat, study or attend concerts, quizzes and lectures. Rooms can also be booked for band rehearsals, workshops or business meetings.

Meanwhile, in the **Lithuanian** capital of Vilnius, a prison has been converted into a cultural hub home to music events, studios and workshops, hosting more than 250 artists. And in **Italy**'s city of Turin, three buildings (including a small castle) that have been confiscated from the mafia are being converted into social welfare spaces offering support to disadvantaged groups.

Creating age-friendly environments

The world's population is ageing, with the proportion of older people in nearly every country growing rapidly. Accordingly, Utopian cities must be designed to support the elderly in continuing to lead vibrant lifestyles. In **Hong Kong**, where life expectancy is the highest in the world, nearly all districts belong to the World Health Organisation's international network of 'age-friendly cities'. These are cities that prioritise features which support older people, such as:

- Sidewalks that are well-maintained and lit up
- Plenty of well-placed and well-maintained public benches
- Adequate, clean and safe public toilets that are easy to locate and accessible by individuals with disabilities
- Housing within the community that supports the needs of older people
- Enough public and retail services close to where people live
- Public buildings that can be accessed easily by individuals with disabilities
- Buses that offer priority seating to the elderly and ensure they are seated before moving
- Adequate reserved parking spots for individuals with disabilities
- Welcoming, individualised service instead of automated answering facilities
- Simply written and clearly legible information
- A civic culture that includes and respects older people

As part of its efforts to create an age-friendly environment, the Hong Kong government conducted a programme inviting older people to report issues they encounter with footpaths and other mobility concerns, for officials to resolve.

Hong Kong is also greener than most cities, according to Dr Timothy Kwok, professor of geriatric medicine at the Chinese University of Hong Kong. He describes how, in the early hours, it's common to see groups of older people spending time in green spaces doing tai chi or qi gong callisthenics, after which they would share meals and chat.

7
Poverty Alleviation

Lives of dignity for all

*"Economic growth doesn't mean anything
unless it is inclusive growth."*
John Green, American author and philanthropist

Utopia would be a place where no person has to struggle to meet their basic needs because of their economic situation or background. What would it take to make this zero-poverty world a reality?

Let's take a look at the strategies that various countries are adopting to achieve human dignity and security today – from leveraging taxation effectively to providing basic resources upfront to adopting targeted measures to aid the disadvantaged.

USING TAXATION TO MEET BASIC NEEDS

Putting taxes to work

"The future is already here –
it's just not very evenly distributed."
William Gibson, American-Canadian writer

As we saw in the chapter on *Happiness*, the citizens of **Denmark** all contribute towards ensuring that the poorest members of society are able to meet a decent standard of living. They do this by paying a significant share of their income in taxes. The middle class pays about 35% to 48% while the richest could even pay 57%. They also pay 25% value-added tax (a form of sales tax) on purchases.

All these taxes go towards ensuring a good standard of living for everyone across society. Citizens may purchase fewer non-essential items and luxuries (which can be quite expensive in Denmark), but they also enjoy more social services and can feel confident that their essential needs will be met, from education to healthcare to parental leave to financial security if they wish to change careers. The social safety net also keeps Danes safe by ensuring there is far less poverty and inequality and, therefore, much less inclination towards crime.

When compared with the United States, those in the bottom third of the income distribution have more disposable income. The opposite is true for the more advantaged in society. This model works well for Denmark since the value of each additional dollar can contribute more to the wellbeing of the poorest than the richest. While having less cash than the average American, the typical Dane enjoys more public services and more time.

Children are key beneficiaries of the tax system. For example, in Helsinki, **Finland**, another country which leverages high taxation to provide exceptional public services, children receive free school meals. Meanwhile, every summer for the past 80 years, all children below the age of 16 can receive a free lunch every weekday from about 40 playgrounds around the city, and hundreds of kids participate.

As we saw in the *Happiness* chapter, paying high taxes doesn't seem to reduce happiness when it translates to great living standards. Most Danes consider it a collective responsibility to work if you can and pay taxes to provide a social safety net to support the very young, the very old, the poor and the sick. Europeans tend to believe that the poor are poor because they have been unlucky rather than lazy.

Delivering efficient public services

Efficiency is a priority of the **Danish** political economy, where there is a keen focus on spotting and eliminating waste. This focus on ongoing improvement boosts the quality of public services and makes citizens more inclined to pay for them. As a result, skilled Danes do not flee the country to avoid high taxes and corporations continue to do business there.

> *"A developed country is not a place where the poor have cars. It's where the rich use public transportation."*
> *Gustavo Petro, president of Colombia*

Since Denmark is a small nation of 5.6 million people, Danes can see and directly receive the benefits of their tax dollars, rather than those dollars being spent in far-off areas where they cannot see how well the money was spent. This further encourages citizens to support the tax system.

Improving tax collection

Some governments have boosted tax revenue by taking steps to improve the process of tax collection. For example, the **Australian** government sends taxpaying citizens pre-filled tax return forms based on the data the authorities have about their income. This makes paying taxes more convenient for citizens as it saves them time and accounting fees. As far back as 1999, 87% of **Danish** taxpayers and 74% of **Swedish** taxpayers used pre-filled tax returns.

Another way to improve tax collection is to switch from chastising the public for evading taxes and instead frame the payment of taxes as a noble act that serves the community. Author Alain De Botton recommends that public services like schools, ambulances and fire engines could carry messages of appreciation towards the tax-paying public, thus encouraging generosity among all.

OFFERING HOUSING FIRST

Treating a roof as a right

A person could end up homeless for many reasons, from sudden unemployment to serious substance abuse to a family split to mental health issues. While most support programmes assume they must first fix those issues before obtaining a permanent home, **Finland** does the opposite.

Finland's Housing First scheme was set up on the basis that it is far easier to solve health and social issues when one has access to a permanent home. Therefore, those who would otherwise be homeless are provided with housing on a standard lease, paying rent as usual.

They may contribute to the cost of support, based on their income, and the balance is taken care of by the local government. To provide the homes to make this initiative possible, Finland used prevailing social housing while buying private flats and building housing blocks from scratch.

Residents also gain customised support including consultations with housing advisors who can guide them if they face rent payment issues or provide advice on securing other government benefits. Counselling on financial management and debt is also available, and residents can often access support within their homes. Compared with the resulting costs to the government of an individual being homeless, the nation saves up to USD 9,600 per person per year by providing homes. It is also better equipped to break the cycle of generational poverty, increasing the prospects of future generations.

In Finland, having a roof over one's head is seen as a human right rather than a privilege to be earned. The country has effectively reduced its homeless population from about 20,000 in the 1980s to about 4,300 in 2021, and seeks to entirely eradicate homelessness by 2025. In addition, every year since 2002, the Finnish capital Helsinki hosts a 'Homeless Night' where citizens donate sleeping bags, clothing, sanitary products, vitamins and other essentials to residents without homes.

Singapore is often recognised as having the best public housing programme in the world, with over 80% of its population residing in flats built by the government. When the nation began to face overcrowding, especially in tightly packed slums, it set up the Housing Development Board in 1960, providing safe, clean and well-maintained flats to house thousands of residents. It later offered subsidised housing for as little as SGD 4,900 (about USD 3,550) on a 99-year lease, with buyers prevented from reselling homes for at least five years. Since 1989, the blocks of flats also require minimum occupancy quotas for

Chinese, Malay and Indian residents, ensuring racial integration. Today, over 3 million residents live in Singapore's good-quality public housing.

Canada similarly has a National Housing Strategy providing affordable housing for the benefit of older people, indigenous families and individuals escaping domestic violence. And the city of Copenhagen in **Denmark** announced in 2022 that 40% of future residential development must be social housing.

The **Austrian** capital of Vienna is considering a creative approach to increasing the supply of affordable housing – by introducing a tax on vacant apartments. This would further incentivise property owners to rent out available spaces, retaining Vienna's reputation as a city of affordable housing.

Providing resources to the homeless

The city of Albuquerque, New Mexico in the **United States** is also actively supporting the homeless with a housing first programme that has reduced unsheltered homelessness by 80% and chronic homelessness by 40%. It has saved taxpayers over USD 5 million while housing 650 people. Signs were placed at 30 intersections displaying a hotline number to call to be directed to shelter, food and services – thousands made the call.

But the mayor did not stop there. He also introduced a citywide initiative to provide day jobs to the unemployed, enlisting their help with cleaning up the city – picking up trash, weeds and litter across 400 city blocks. More than 200 people were subsequently connected to full-time employment. In the mayor's words, "There's always something to do – weeds to pull, litter to pick up. (...) So, if you have something to do and you need people that need something to do, there's a better way."

Similarly, the city of Santa Cruz de Tenerife in **Spain** has offered employment in cleaning and gardening the city's small green spaces to

100 people experiencing long-term unemployment. They will also receive job training and certificates of competencies and qualifications.

The **Greek** capital of Athens is also making efforts to care for its homeless population. In 2020, it set up a Multipurpose Homeless Centre which can house 400 people, providing shelter as well as food, washing machines, showers and internet facilities. The site is also staffed with doctors, social workers and mental health professionals. The city further boasts a modern hair salon offering free haircuts to those in need and 'street work' teams who tend to the needs of those who continue to live on the streets.

In 2021, Athens went further and adopted a 'Homeless Bill of Rights' which recognises that all people have a fundamental right to housing, employment, education and health. The city has now introduced an intensive training programme to provide interested homeless centre residents with employment-related skills, as well as support in writing CVs and preparing for interviews.

Meanwhile, cities like Ghent in **Belgium** and Berlin in **Germany** are sending patrols onto the streets to check on homeless citizens during times of need. During the heat waves in Ghent in 2022, patrols sought out vulnerable residents to check if they needed medical help and provide them with water to prevent dehydration. Similarly, in Berlin, 'cold buses' roamed the streets during the 2021 winter months providing hot tea and sleeping bags, or driving individuals to homeless shelters. The number of beds at emergency overnight facilities was doubled to accommodate those in need.

PROVIDING CASH INJECTIONS

Providing grants to those in need

Brazil is known to have one of the best poverty reduction programmes in the world, reducing extreme poverty by 16% and income inequality by 25%. The programme has been so effective that nearly 20 other countries have adapted and implemented it.

Direct cash transfers are provided to families in need as a monthly grant distributed to the female adult of the family. In turn, the families commit to keeping their children in school and taking them for regular health checks. In this way, the programme helps to break the cycle of intergenerational poverty. Compared with non-beneficiaries, those who receive family grants see greater school attendance and progression among children. Pregnant women receive more prenatal care, have babies of higher birth weights and children are more likely to be vaccinated. Infant mortality has dropped, especially since malnutrition fell by 65%. Adults who received the grant were more likely to participate in the labour market, particularly women, and child labour reduced.

Individuals who are elderly or have disabilities also receive a continuous cash benefit. This is of much higher value than the family grant programme provides, essentially equal to a minimum wage. It is far more effective in combatting poverty, though it reaches fewer families and is more expensive to provide.

Driving education forward

Families in poverty often cannot afford to send their children to school as the child's labour is essential for the family to scrape by each day. Recognising this, **Mexico** began paying families to send children to school. The goal was to break the cycle of intergenerational poverty transmission. The older a child was, the more they were generally paid, offsetting the amounts they would typically earn for the family. Payments were given to mothers to manage, with slightly more paid out for girls since girls were more likely to be made to drop out of school.

"If you stick me down in the middle of Bangladesh or Peru or someplace, you find out how much this talent is going to produce in the wrong kind of soil."
Warren Buffet, business magnate, investor and philanthropist

Nearly 6 million families were assisted by the programme, with more children going to school and staying in school longer. Within 20 years of the programme beginning, Mexico achieved gender parity in education, including at high school and college levels. The country also has the world's highest percentage of female computer science degree holders. Fifty-two nations have introduced their own variations of Mexico's programme.

Investing in Universal Basic Income

Alaska in the **United States** enjoys a significant return from investing the tens of billions in revenue it has accumulated from its oil reserves over the past decades. The governor of Alaska claims that the state's natural resource wealth ultimately belongs to its people. Accordingly, since 1982, every Alaskan who has resided there for at least a year and intends to keep living there, and who has not been in jail in the past year, receives a cheque of up to USD 2,000 every year, irrespective of their income. On average, each household receives about USD 4,000 annually.

The Alaskan people, only 24% of whom identify as liberal, embrace the fund. 84% of citizens support it being paid to all residents and 62% say that the government, even in a crisis, should never touch the fund for any other use. A greater number of Alaskans say it has boosted their incentive to work rather than reducing it. This is supported by the fact that from the 1980s to the 2000s, the only US state where the incomes of the bottom 20% increased faster than the incomes of the top 20%, was Alaska.

Such a system of guaranteed income can help to eradicate poverty. The town of Dauphin in **Canada** made it happen by guaranteeing all its residents a basic income to ensure that each one was above the poverty line. To finance the initiative, Dauphin used a 'negative income tax' which supplemented the incomes of residents if they ever fell below the poverty line. As a result, residents saw improved school performance and lower dropout rates, and a reduction in hospitalisation rates of as much as 8.5%. Mental health and domestic violence complaints fell. Moreover, residents continued to work, with only new mothers and students working a bit less.

Other studies affirm that basic income neither incentivises nor discourages work – work is generally more than a mere source of income to most people, providing life with purpose and meaning. The health and education benefits of such an initiative have shown up in US studies as well, while a trial in **Finland** demonstrated improvements in wellbeing, reducing depression and boosting life satisfaction.

Dutch historian Rutger Bregman argues that, for many countries, funding a similar effort is not a pipe dream. He describes how a net cost of USD 175 billion, which represents 1% of the USA's GDP and a quarter of its military spending, would ensure that no US citizen faces poverty.

Many countries have started performing experiments in providing a universal basic income, including **Brazil**, **Canada**, **Denmark**, **Finland**,

India, Kenya, Namibia, the **Netherlands** and the **USA**, while countries such as France, Germany and Scotland have begun designing such programmes.

In **Ireland**, the government is using the concept to support its arts sector by offering a basic income for artists, giving about 2,000 artists around USD 250 per week for three years with no strings attached. The deputy prime minister has also proposed to replace the minimum wage with a 'living wage' that can ensure a decent standard of living – defined as 60% of the median wage.

DEPLOYING STRATEGIC RELIEF

Providing targeted support

Considering a poverty line of USD 1.90 a day, over the 32 years from 1981 to 2013, **China** lifted 850 million people out of poverty, bringing down its poverty rate from 88% to under 2%. How did China achieve this remarkable feat?

Over USD 80 billion was spent on poverty alleviation efforts. Clear goals were established for poverty reduction and more than 775,000 officers were dispatched to survey rural populations. A first-of-its-kind database of all individuals experiencing poverty was developed, with data on every person, household and village, and an officer was assigned to monitor each household's progress. Seven institutions were set up to handle registration/accountability, policy, investment, assistance, social mobilisation, multi-channel 360-degree supervision, and assessment.

Millions of households were relocated from remote villages to newly constructed ones better suited to economic growth. Roads, houses, schools and other facilities were constructed, and direct unconditional cash transfers (known as *dibao*) and interest-free loans were provided.

Apart from relocation, industrial development, social security and education, eco-compensation was also used. This involved incentivising farmers and local governments with direct payments for reforestation, soil conservation and revegetation efforts. Citizens supported the efforts by making donations and assisting farmers in selling produce. Health workers were also dispatched to rural communities to provide medical check-ups and offer treatment.

In 2021, the country reported that extreme poverty had been eradicated, considering a threshold of USD 1.69 a day.

"Zero is the only acceptable percentage
of extreme poverty."
Alicia Bárcena Ibarra, Executive Secretary
of the United Nations Economic Commission

Like China, **Vietnam** dramatically reduced extreme poverty rates over a similar period. In fact, it was able to achieve the Millennium Development Goal of halving its poverty rate a decade before the UN deadline. In 30 years, 40 million Vietnamese were lifted out of poverty.

Programmes that helped to make this happen included providing free health insurance to children and their families, and supporting children's education with tuition exceptions, subsidies and loans. Vietnam also actively supported the needs of ethnic minorities who are at greater risk of facing poverty. With the help of the World Bank, the country aided farmers in growing more profitable crops and boosted farming productivity by developing farmers' skills. Through such efforts, almost 1.5 million Vietnamese transition into the middle class every year, and poverty levels have dropped to around 10%.

Creating entrepreneurs

Women are most impacted by poverty, and also most likely to take action to escape it, and help their families do so too. The world's largest NGO, **Bangladesh**-founded BRAC, has used this information to successfully support nearly nine million people out of poverty. The programme works by, over a two-year period, providing cash or food to meet a woman's survival needs, then providing her with an asset such as livestock and training on how to use it for income generation and financial education, and finally supporting social integration among other women entrepreneurs and her community. Seven years after joining the programme, 92% of women had maintained or grown their income and assets. In fact, Nobel prize-winning economists have identified the programme as one of the most successful efforts to break the poverty cycle.

Empowering individuals through entrepreneurship can also enhance public safety by giving at-risk youth an alternative to the promises of wealth and security offered by recruiting gangs and violent groups. Thus, investment in entrepreneurship education and incubators can generate significant public savings by indirectly fighting crime.

Introducing childhood interventions

Interventions targeting children can have dramatic results. For example, a 20-year study in **Jamaica** found that the simple act of providing babies and small children with simple, handmade toys (picture cards, dolls made out of socks, cars made of plastic bottles) resulted in a 25% increase in earnings later in life. Early childhood stimulation, engagement and education go a long way.

Social integration matters too. A 2007 study in Connecticut in the **United States** discovered that low-income students in economically mixed prekindergarten classes advanced in critical language skills over the school year. They improved from significantly below the national average to slightly above it. This was not the case for children in classes limited to low-income students, which remained below average. The better-off students, meanwhile, did neither better nor worse.

Other efforts target older youth. For example, the '93% club' in the **United Kingdom** aims to support the 93% of students who attend public schools (as opposed to private schools). It provides them with mentorship from individuals from top corporations, takes professional headshots for their LinkedIn profiles, and offers general support and guidance as they enter the working world.

Encouraging saving

Individuals who depend on daily wages to get through the day can often fall into difficulty when they face an unexpected expense. To help prevent the resultant downward spiral, villagers in Kibera in **Kenya** were encouraged to save money for emergencies. Psychologist Dan Ariely found that sending them weekly reminders by text message helped, and more so when the text messages were worded as though they were coming from their child.

However, what was twice as effective was providing villagers with a physical token to scratch to indicate whether they had saved or not that week. This seemed to provide an alternative ritual to perform in place of what they would otherwise have done while spending money. This behavioural psychology tactic successfully doubled savings rates.

8
Governance
Faith in a fair system

*"Politics should be directed as the great sages
long ago insisted: to the wellbeing of the people,
not the power of the rulers."*
Jeffrey Sachs, co-editor of the World Happiness Report

The citizens of Utopia would have trust and confidence in the system of governance operating in their daily lives. They would expect a corruption-free government that they could respect, with principles of equity and justice clearly practised. Where can we look for insights on how to get there?

Transparency International's Corruption Perceptions Index rates and ranks 180 countries based on their perceived levels of public sector corruption by experts and businesspeople. **Denmark** claims the top spot on the Index of 2022, with a score of 90 out of 100. **Finland** and **New Zealand** follow, with scores of 87, while **Norway** (84), **Singapore** (83) and **Sweden** (83) are also top scorers, followed by **Switzerland** (82). Let's discover how these nations came to win the trust of their citizens.

SHARING LEADERSHIP

Governing collectively

New Zealand follows a Mixed Member Proportional (MMP) voting system. Under this system, each citizen can vote for a local member of parliament and also for a preferred political party. Parties are then represented in parliament based on the share of votes the party received. This system makes it unlikely that one party will dominate the seats in parliament – usually, the party with the most votes needs to form a coalition with another party or parties in order to govern.

> *"Let us not seek the Republican answer or*
> *the Democratic answer, but the right answer.*
> *Let us not seek to fix the blame for the past.*
> *Let us accept our own responsibility for the future."*
> *John F. Kennedy, 35th president of the United States*

Consensus is a hallmark of politics in **Denmark** as well. The parliament comprises representatives from 14 parties. As no individual party has had enough of the 179 votes to run by itself, multi-party coalitions have been formed to govern collectively since 1909. The parties negotiate on goals, and typically, a key person from one of the stronger parties in the coalition will become the prime minister, while leaders from other coalition parties may take key ministerial posts in justice, finance and foreign affairs.

Switzerland takes shared leadership to another level – its president shares equal power with six additional people. Swiss citizens elect their federal parliament which then selects seven people from among them to serve as something akin to ministers. Those individuals then share power, with each one taking a turn acting as Switzerland's international representative for a year (technically the president for the year). However, that person shares equal power with the rest and the team collectively makes decisions.

All these governments show a willingness to share power and leadership, valuing collaboration over egocentricity.

Ensuring diversity of representation

New Zealand boasts the world's most diverse parliament. The mixed-member-proportional (MMP) electoral system introduced in 1996 is credited by analysts for the diversity seen. Indeed, the New Zealand parliament includes close to 50% female representation (highest among the OECD nations), Māori, Pasifika and Asian parliamentarians, the first MP of African origin and second refugee, Ibrahim Omer, and Vanushi Walters, of Sri Lankan origin.

Rather than being tokens for diversity, these individuals hold positions of power. Among the 20-member cabinet, eight members are women and a quarter are Māori. The 11% of LGBTQIA+ lawmakers (believed to be the world's highest proportion) include the deputy prime minister. The country also has its first indigenous female Foreign Minister who wears a traditional Māori face tattoo. Describing this parliament, Jennifer Curtin, director of the Public Policy Institute at the University of Auckland said: "It looks like New Zealand looks. We're not male, pale and stale anymore."

Upon officially opening in 2020, the oath of allegiance was recited in 10 languages, besides the official English and te reo Māori languages. In 2017, references to specific deities were removed from the parliamentary prayer to make room for religious inclusivity. Additionally, accommodations for parents have improved – the Speaker of the House, Trevor Mallard, has even gone viral for bottle-feeding a parliamentarian's baby mid-debate!

The parliament of **Sweden** boasts a wide age range – with parliamentarians appointed in 2018 being as young as 22 and as old as 85. Meanwhile, **New Zealand** appointed Jacinda Ardern in 2017 (37 years when appointed prime minister), and **Ukraine** appointed Oleksiy Honcharuk in 2019 (35 years when appointed prime minister).

Diversity in leadership helps to build trust among the public, who gain greater confidence that their interests will be represented. **Finland** has made progress in terms of age, gender and socioeconomic background. In 2019, Sanna Marin became the world's youngest serving state leader at the age of 34. The prime minister has expressed her pride in her country, where the child of a poor family can secure an education and realise their life goals. A family background that would appear scandalous in other countries – featuring her father's alcoholism, parents' divorce and mother's same-sex relationship – didn't dissuade the Finnish citizenry from voting for Marin, who was the first in her family to go to university. Indeed, Marin's government has enjoyed some of Finland's highest approval ratings – over 70% in 2020. Three of her key ministers are also female and under the age of 35, namely the minister of finance, minister of education and minister of interior.

Finland's five major parties are all led by women, and the nation is also in the unusual position of having more women on its cabinet than men – women represent 12 portfolios, while men represent seven. As of 2019, women accounted for 47% of the country's parliamentarians. How has Finland achieved this level of representation? Among other factors, the World Bank Group demonstrates a significant correlation between the provision of robust childcare support and a boost of 25% or more to women's representation in national parliaments.

Relying on experts

The **Danish** parliament evaluates 200-300 proposed bills per year. Standing committees confer about proposals and secure the views of experts, scholars and representatives from interest groups. Time is allowed for deliberation – only after reflecting on these views does the parliament make a decision on whether or not to pass the bill.

Trustworthy governments have the humility to defer to other authorities. When the COVID-19 pandemic hit, the prime minister of **New Zealand** Jacinda Arden rapidly sought the advice of epidemiologists and decisively put their guidance into practice. Her capacity to acknowledge where external expertise was needed went a long way towards safeguarding citizens' lives.

CULTIVATING CIVIC ENGAGEMENT

Encouraging regular voting

Well-governed countries usually have engaged citizens who vote regularly in democratic elections and make their voices heard. In **Denmark**, elections occur at least every four years, while in **New Zealand**, they occur every 3 years.

Swiss citizens, meanwhile, have the right to vote every four months, indicating their views on all nationwide and state-level laws proposed over the prior four months. In this way, citizens don't merely select their leadership, they also choose their policies.

Referendums empowering the public to challenge decisions of parliament require just 50,000 signatures to be put to a nationwide vote – 100,000 if the law in question affects the constitution. Indeed, the majority of laws are introduced via popular vote. Turnout for referendums averages an impressive 46%, with 66% of voters having shown up to vote on a COVID-19 referendum.

In the **United Kingdom**, any resident or citizen can directly petition the government about a law or policy via an e-petitions website and, if over 10,000 people sign, the government must make a formal response. If over 100,000 people sign, the petition will be considered for debate in parliament.

Mandating civic duties

Since individual citizens may feel that their solitary vote will have little impact on election outcomes and may seek to bypass any inconvenience associated with voting, many may fail to vote for their preferred candidate. As a result, the eventual outcome may not be representative of most citizens' preferences. **Australia**, however, sees an impressive level of voter turnout – 91% in recent elections. Contrast this with the OECD average of 68%.

> *"One of the penalties for refusing to participate in politics is that you end up being governed by your inferiors."*
> *Plato, Greek philosopher*

The reason behind this high degree of civic participation is Australia's mandatory voting policy. Every eligible Australian must register and cast a ballot (even an unfilled one). If not, they will receive a mail asking them why they did not do so and be fined a small amount, about USD 14 (though this can go up to USD 57). This practice narrows the gap between voter turnout among the wealthy and the poor – the difference in voting behaviour between the top and bottom 20% in terms of wealth is 13% on average across the OECD, but only 6% in Australia. In this way, the practice accounts for the preferences of those at the lower end of the socioeconomic spectrum.

Further encouraging voting, Australian elections are always held on Saturdays to minimise interference with work. Voters can also mail in ballots or vote in person ahead of the election day.

Making voting more inclusive

In **Canada**, most citizens are automatically registered to vote when they turn 18, eliminating the hassle of voluntary registration processes. Voters can simply turn up at the polls and place their vote. By doing away with bureaucratic red tape, Canada makes civic participation that much easier.

Luxembourg has abolished the requirement for foreign nationals to have been residents in the country for five years before being able to vote in local elections, recognising that this requirement prevented about a third of its resident population from participating in the democratic process. Now, all residents who register with the municipality may vote.

Meanwhile, a few countries, including **Austria**, **Belgium**, **Greece** and **Malta**, have also reduced the voting age. From 2024, Belgium will permit residents over the age of 16 to vote in EU elections. The goal is to give youth – who are the future – the opportunity to shape that future. This decision helped earn the Belgian city of Ghent the title of 'European Youth Capital 2024'.

Activating citizen voices

Several countries, including **Canada**, **Ireland**, the **Netherlands**, **Poland** and the **United Kingdom**, use citizen assemblies to inclusively engage citizens in decision-making. These forums invite a random selection of citizens to arrive at a conclusion on policy issues that affect them through a process of learning, deliberation and decision-making. The process engages a representative sample of the public while using expert education and deliberation to combat misinformation and ignorance. The group's recommendations are then forwarded to the local authority for potential implementation.

In Brasov, **Romania**, a Children's Council has been set up featuring 20 children aged 11 to 17 who will provide a voice in municipal policy. The youth are selected ensuring diversity of gender, socioeconomic background, disability, institutionalisation, etc.

Urban forums also enable citizens to participate in decision-making. For example, the **Spanish** city of Valencia organised a round table event to discuss how to make the city more inclusive for women, culminating in a roadmap for building a more egalitarian city. Meanwhile, the **Czech** city of Pilsen engaged aspiring business owners in using an entrepreneurial process of 'design thinking' to generate innovative solutions to resolve complaints by the city's residents.

Social media has a role as well. The **Danish** municipality of Guldborgsund is using technology to boost political engagement, making it easier for citizens to follow political discussions and decision-making by broadcasting its city council meetings live on Facebook.

Practising participatory budgeting

Many cities are engaging citizens in the powerful process of participatory budgeting. In this process, citizens can submit proposals for their city's development and also vote on all submissions. The city then funds and implements those proposals with the highest votes.

The city of Brasov in **Romania** has used participatory budgeting to make its citizens' ideas a reality, with the areas of mobility, leisure, greenery and communities being allocated a budget of about USD 100,000 each. Winning ideas included provisions for community gardens and outdoor musical instruments. In the city of Bucharest, citizens proposed projects ranging from improved cycling infrastructure to a site for donations to disadvantaged children.

Meanwhile, the first participatory budget in Budapest, **Hungary** resulted in 15 projects being allocated around USD 2.9 million collectively. Winning projects include renovating and renting out municipal flats to homeless individuals, introducing a leisure centre for people with autism, and cultivating small urban forests. The **Belgian** town of Beerse also has a budget of about USD 40,000 in place dedicated to projects proposed by youth aged 12 to 25.

In this way, participatory budgeting empowers citizens to engage in direct democracy, making their ideas for their community a reality.

Conducting democracy festivals

*"You have not converted a man
because you have silenced him."
John Morley, British statesman and writer*

The Nordic countries, including **Denmark**, **Norway**, **Sweden** and **Finland**, initiated the concept of democracy festivals – colourful events to facilitate constructive political dialogue. Free and open to everyone, democracy festivals aim to foster a culture of open discussion, debate and critical thinking. Generally held in the summer and featuring food and music, they bring together activists, politicians, entrepreneurs and citizens of diverse ages, genders, opinions and backgrounds to sit together and talk about how to make the country a better place to live.

BUILDING A JUST SOCIETY

Accounting for second choices

When there are multiple similar candidates, the majority's vote can become split such that a candidate who is less preferred can win an election despite securing only a minority of votes. To avoid this, **Australia** makes use of a system of "preferential voting". This requires voters to specify their order of preference among the candidates (1st, 2nd, 3rd, etc.). Then, if no one candidate secures a majority of the vote, the candidate with the least number of first-choice votes is dropped and the second-choice votes of their supporters are redistributed among the remaining candidates. The process continues until one of the candidates secures a majority. This system takes into consideration the preferences of those whose first-choice candidates are unlikely to win.

Protecting independent judicial systems

Finland has been recognised by the World Economic Forum in 2019 as having the world's most independent judicial system. As in **New Zealand**, power is shared across the parliament (which makes the law), the judiciary (which interprets the law via the courts) and the government (which administers the law). In **Denmark**, the independence of the judiciary from the government and parliament is enshrined in the constitution.

Denmark also has a parliamentary ombudsman – a parliament-appointed lawyer who serves as a watchdog over government-controlled institutions to protect citizen rights. Prisons and psychiatric hospitals are frequently inspected, public buildings are monitored for disability accessibility, the deporting of foreign nationals is supervised, and citizens' complaints are investigated. The ombudsman can criticise the government and ask the courts to raise cases against the government if laws are being violated. The official Danish ombudsman website states: "The Ombudsman cannot demand that the authorities follow a recommendation – however, in practice they always do."

Ensuring transparency

Transparency is an important factor that has led **Denmark** to consistently hold the top spot in the Corruption Perception Index. There is a high degree of press freedom, and information on public expenditure is freely available.

Technology helps boost transparency. In 2019, Denmark pledged to provide justice sector employees (across prosecutions, police, security and intelligence, prisons and justice ministry) with an anonymous whistle-blower system to report any concerns. It also pledged to provide citizens with an online platform to access all the data that the government holds about them.

The **Croatian** city of Pula plans to become 100% transparent, making every last penny spent with public money visible to the public through a digital application called iTransparency. Meanwhile, **Bulgaria** intends to award 'zero corruption' certificates to municipalities that introduce comprehensive transparency measures to combat corruption, with independent control by Transparency International. The country's Anti-Corruption Fund has also introduced a web platform for anonymous tips on corruption and misuse of funds.

In the **United Kingdom**, citizens can obtain the contact details of local MPs from the parliament website. They can also visit theyworkforyou.com to check the voting records of their MPs and learn where they stand on important issues.

Avoiding tipping culture

Intriguingly, Harvard Business School research has revealed a strong correlation between the level of tipping in a country and the level of corruption in that country. The study suggests that bribes can be similar to tips by rewarding advantageous service, one before and the other after the service is provided.

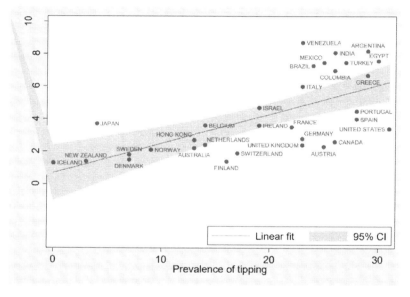

Country-level association between tipping and corruption; Source: Magnus Thor Torfason, Francis J. Flynn, and Daniella Kupor

Building a culture of accountability

When **British** prime minister Rishi Sunak shared a video in which he was not wearing a seatbelt in a moving car, he was fined by Lancashire police. While the fine amount is nominal, the action clearly conveys that the rule of law applies to all.

In 2018, the president of the **Philippines**, Rodrigo Duterte, as part of efforts to stamp out corruption, oversaw the destruction of 76 luxury cars and motorcycles which had been smuggled into the country. The crushing of the Lamborghini, Mercedes-Benz and Porsche vehicles by bulldozer was filmed and circulated nationwide.

MINIMISING CRIME

> *"A society should be judged not by how it treats its outstanding citizens but by how it treats its criminals."*
> *Fyodor Dostoyevsky, Russian novelist*

Cultivating good neighbours

Norway has seen an impressive reduction in the rate of re-offence among prisoners – a drop from about 65% in the 1990s to just 20% – the world's lowest. What is Norway's secret for creating a safer society? It boils down to a focus on 'cultivating good neighbours'.

Norway believes that taking away a prisoner's freedom is punishment enough, and therefore, instead of striving to exact 'revenge' and mistreat prisoners, the country endeavours to rehabilitate them so they will be good neighbours and contributing citizens once released. Norwegian prison governor Are Hoidal explains: "If we treat inmates like animals in prison, then we will release animals onto your street." This tallies with research from the United States Department of Justice, which found that strict incarceration actually increases re-offence rates. Meanwhile, facilities that include cognitive-behavioural programmes grounded in social learning theory work best to keep former prisoners out of trouble.

Training for future vocations

In **Norwegian** prisons, the emphasis is on education, with the goal of giving rehabilitated prisoners an avenue to rebuild their lives beyond selling drugs or resorting to crime. Programmes and courses such as woodworking are provided, along with access to studios and an on-site garage. Prisoners have expressed a sense of pride and accomplishment they had never felt before on realising they could master diverse new skills and contribute something to others. Many will be released as fully qualified carpenters, mechanics and chefs. One inmate has spent his time in prison publishing a cookbook, securing a diploma in graphic design, successfully completing multiple exams, and studying physics.

Such efforts work in other countries too. A prison in Kampala, **Uganda**, has one of the world's lowest re-offence rates – all thanks to its education and rehabilitation programmes. Meanwhile, in **Singapore**'s women's prison, inmates get training in hairdressing, baking or using Microsoft Office. Similarly, a women's prison in Surrey in the **United Kingdom** provides classes in beauty treatment and cosmetology. At another facility in Surrey, prisoners were trained to make baked goods – by the famed chef Gordon Ramsay himself! Filming the effort as a television show called *Gordon Behind Bars*, Ramsay aimed to help make prisoners more employable upon release. Their products were sold to local cafés and eateries under the brand and slogan 'Bad Boy Bakery: Life-changing Taste'.

Providing a calm environment

Prisoners in **Norway** used to spend the majority of the day locked up, but the country has changed its once hard approach. Prisoners now leave their cells at 7:30 am, begin work at 8:15 am, and spend only one hour during the day locked in their cells (coinciding with the prison officers' break time) before being locked in again at 8:30 pm.

The jail cells are more akin to small dormitory rooms, with confining bars banned in many prisons. Prisoners can wear their own clothes. Prison officers don't carry guns or pepper spray, though they do have personal alarms. Making the environment as natural as possible does make a difference – the inmates' behaviour changes have helped boost their rates of employment.

Employing trained prison officers

In **Norway**, becoming a prison officer requires two to three years of university training, with 175 trainees selected from more than 1,200 applicants each year. Prison officers (half of whom are female in order to mimic the world outside) engage in activities alongside prisoners, from eating to leisure activities like playing volleyball. They chat with and motivate prisoners, serving as role models, mentors and coaches.

Busying prisoners with activities

At prisons in **Norway**, classes such as yoga are available to promote peaceful thinking and behaviour. Many facilities in the **United States** have also introduced activities to help inmates manage their tempers and keep busy. A facility in Pennsylvania that offers game rooms and craft centres boasts some of the lowest rates of prison violence across the state. Another in Wisconsin provides art and painting lessons to reduce stress. In one facility in Minnesota, non-violent offenders are engaged in stained-glass creation and leather-making, while at another, inmates can rent instruments such as guitars, drums and a piano. Meanwhile, a prison in Virginia offers family activities like father-daughter dances.

In the **United Kingdom**, a prison in Wandsworth has two gyms and a sports hall, and inmates have created an award-winning radio programme that has even interviewed Hugh Jackman. Meanwhile, in Cebu, **Philippines**, a prison has gone viral for its unique rehabilitation programme. Here, prisoners choreograph complex dance routines to musical numbers like 'Thriller' and 'Gangnam Style'. In Bialystok, **Poland**, inmates renovate kennels for dogs at the local shelter.

Offering supportive services

In the **United Kingdom**, 57% of women prisoners have reported being victims of domestic abuse. Nearly half say their offence was committed to support another's drug use. And self-harm is almost five times greater in women's prisons. Considering all these factors, the country has invested millions of pounds in providing support to women prisoners to address substance misuse and mental health issues. **Singapore**'s women's prison also provides its inmates with two-hour group counselling sessions three times a week.

Reducing prison sentences

Nearly everyone in a **Norwegian** prison will eventually be released – the country has banned life sentences, with the maximum sentence set at 21 years, although it can be extended in five-year increments if the individual is still considered a threat to society. Reduced sentences also introduce major savings to the government. Those savings can be redirected towards the rehabilitation of prisoners via education, job training, drug treatment programmes and post-release support.

The United States, for example, where sentence terms are about five times the length of those in European countries, could stand to gain from such a model. Calculations reveal that adopting a European-style system would generate substantial savings – even if the number of crimes committed was double that in Europe. A change in the system could reduce the rate of incarceration and the need to build new prisons. It could also increase post-release employment, and in turn, reduce welfare expenditure and potentially boost tax revenue. Perhaps most importantly, it would result in a safer society with fewer crimes.

Leveraging restorative justice

Restorative justice allows the victims of crimes to meet the person responsible and express how the incident affected them. It also facilitates both parties in arriving at an agreement on how things will be put right. While you might think that victims would not want to meet offenders, when asked by a trained facilitator, most do. In **Northern Ireland**, three-quarters of victims of young offenders choose to meet the young person face to face, and are far more satisfied with the outcome than they are with traditionally punitive processes.

The **United Kingdom** found that 85% of participating victims were satisfied with the restorative justice experience – it allows them to get answers to their questions and increases the chances that they will receive an apology. Importantly, the procedure reduces re-offence rates by 14%-27% as it allows offenders to better understand the harm caused by their actions. The study also found that every £1 spent on restorative justice led to £9 in savings to the criminal justice system by providing an alternative to prosecution and lowering re-offence rates. Directing young offenders to a pre-court restorative justice programme could alone generate savings of nearly £275 million.

Channelling fine money towards victims

In the **Belgian** town of Aalter, all money from traffic fine tickets is channelled towards the victims of traffic accidents. Similarly, in the **United States**, a Crime Victims Fund is available comprised of money from fines imposed on individual and corporate criminals. The fund is used to support the expenses of victims, including medical expenses, lost wages, counselling expenses, etc.

9

Economic Growth

*"The prosperity of a people is proportionate to
the number of hands and minds usefully employed."*
Samuel Johnson, English writer

Utopia would be a prosperous place, with a wealth of resources to serve the needs of its people. Happily, several countries hint at the route to designing a world of economic abundance.

According to the International Monetary Fund, as of 2022, the countries with the highest GDP per capita in the world are **Luxembourg** (USD 128,000), **Ireland** (USD 102,000), **Norway** (USD 93,000), **Switzerland** (USD 92,000), and **Qatar** (USD 83,000). They are followed by Singapore, the United States, Iceland, Australia and Denmark.

These countries reveal that economic success comes from investing in creating a growth-friendly environment. Let's evaluate some common ingredients.

GEARING FOR ECONOMIC GROWTH

Investing in citizens

Among the top 10 wealthiest nations, four of them (**Norway, Switzerland**, the **United States** and **Denmark**) ranked in the top five in the Human Capital Index of 2017. This highlights the link between national wealth and investments in citizen education, employment and skills. The recipe for high GDP per capita seems to be ensuring that as many as possible receive high-quality education and continue that education, enjoy a high rate of employment and gender parity in the workforce, and have the skills to perform high-value work.

In providing free and high-quality education, countries like **Norway** and **Denmark** have succeeded in grooming nations of highly skilled citizens.

> *"The ultimate resource in economic development is people. It is people, not capital or raw materials that develop an economy."*
> *Peter Drucker, Austrian-American management consultant, educator and author*

With the sixth-highest GDP per capita as of 2022, **Singapore**'s economy stands out in Southeast Asia. Unlike other nations in the region, Singapore has never been mainly dependent on producing commodities. Instead, the government has committed to boosting the productivity and value of human capital through a firm focus on education and health. As a result, instead of operating in labour-intensive sectors, Singapore operates in high-tech sectors like electronic manufacturing and the production of precision equipment.

This strategic focus makes it no wonder that the nation topped the 2020 rankings of the Human Capital Index.

Building a strong services sector

Much of **Luxembourg**'s wealth results from a flourishing services sector, including a large financial sector bolstered by favourable tax rules, and information technology and biomedical research industries. Many key EU institutions have set up in the small nation, which provides value-added services that account for nearly 80% of its GDP, as of 2021. In the **United States** as well, the services sector – dominated by fields such as technology, financial services, healthcare and retail – contributes to about 80% of the GDP. And in **Switzerland**, over 70% of its GDP comes from its services sector, including its world-renowned international banking industry.

> *"In Nigeria, financial services, telecoms,*
> *and entertainment have driven growth more than oil."*
> *Oscar N. Onyema, CEO of the Nigerian Stock Exchange*

Singapore, meanwhile, has created a comparative advantage in knowledge-intensive sectors, particularly communications and information and financial services. About 70% of its GDP comes from value-added services. **Iceland**, **Australia** and **Denmark** also leverage the services sector for over 65% of their GDP. And while **Norway** benefits from significant natural resource wealth, the country's services sector still accounts for over half of its GDP.

Establishing a robust export sector

The one country that exports the most goods and services relative to its GDP is **Luxembourg**, with an export sector worth 212% of its GDP, as of 2021. The country focuses on very profitable sectors and uses the profits to import whatever it needs, such as food items (its agricultural sector represents less than 0.3% of its GDP). Luxembourg's top exports are iron products, rubber tires, machinery, plastics and cars.

Singapore also has an impressive export sector, accounting for 185% of its GDP. Machinery and equipment represent its biggest export category, followed by petroleum and chemical products.

Ireland has also used an export-based model to catapult itself from one of the poorest nations in the EU to among the wealthiest. Its export sector represents 135% of its GDP and pharmaceuticals are its top export. **Switzerland** is also well known for its robust export market, where pharmaceuticals, chemicals, machinery, electronics and watches are key contributors. Meanwhile, **Norway**'s export sector is its largest economic contributor by far – with crude petroleum and petroleum gas contributing 40% of the sector's value, and fish and other seafood also playing a big role.

Attracting foreign investment

Favourable tax systems have helped both Ireland and Switzerland attract foreign investment. Many foreign companies have moved their headquarters to **Ireland** to take advantage, further encouraged by the stable business environment, skilled and English-speaking labour force, and strong relations with the United States. Further incentivising investors, Dublin is set to offer free public Wi-Fi throughout the city as part of its Smart Dublin programme.

Switzerland, meanwhile, has long attracted businesses and high-net-worth individuals due to its tax system, dramatically growing national wealth and establishing one of the largest financial centres in the world. The country has one of the highest concentrations of multinational headquarters – almost 30,000 multinationals have a presence, with over

16,000 having set up their headquarters there. Having few rules associated with investment makes the country a top choice among foreign investors. China, for example, invested USD 40 billion in all of the EU in 2016, while investing USD 45 billion in Switzerland alone in the same year!

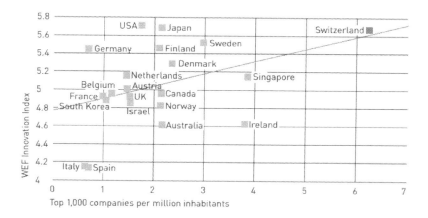

Correlation between multinationals and innovation; Source: economiesuisse, Forbes (listing of 2,000 biggest companies by turnover)

Singapore's economic development has also depended heavily on capital investment from foreign multinationals. The economy was liberalised to attract such investment and free trade zones were set up, alongside other incentives.

Cultivating stability and transparency

Stability is a foundational ingredient to **Switzerland**'s success, supported by the nation's neutral stance in key wars and conflicts. While other nations' economies were ruined, Switzerland sidestepped the biggest destroyer of economic growth – war. The nation's fair and open government, secure and supportive corporate environment, and leading education system all boost its stability. Another wealthy nation, **Sweden**, also boasts a 200-year history of official military neutrality.

> *"We cannot talk about economic development*
> *without talking about peace. How can we expect*
> *economic development in a battlefield?"*
> *Aung San Suu Kyi, Burmese politician*
> *and Nobel Peace Prize laureate*

Alongside being one of the world's least corrupt nations, **Norway**'s low rate of wealth inequality contributes to its economic stability. While the **United States** has a high degree of inequality, it also has the benefit of an established rule of law, deep capital markets and a flexible workforce – all of which factor into its economic stability.

Keeping borders open

Iceland is part of the European Economic Area, which allows individuals belonging to EU member states to cross borders freely for work and reside in any member state. In 2020, immigrants comprised a fifth of Iceland's labour market. As a major part of the country's labour force, immigrants played a key role in Iceland's economic upturn.

The EU's open borders have boosted its economic activity – in 2018, 'mobile' workers were 4% more likely to be employed than the average EU citizen. According to historian Rutger Bregman, opening borders worldwide could boost global wealth by USD 65 trillion by enabling the free flow of human capital. In fact, scientists at the World Bank have reported that if all the world's developed countries would let in just 3% more immigrants, the world's poor would have USD 305 billion more to spend – three times more than the combined total of all development aid.

Bregman has also debunked several myths associated with immigration, for example, showing how immigration expands the labour market, rather than taking jobs away from the local community, and that hardworking immigrants actually boost productivity, generating wealth for everyone. In England, for example, immigrants generate more tax revenue per capita compared with the local population.

ACTIVATING LATENT POTENTIAL

"The world will never realise 100 per cent of its goals if
50 per cent of its people cannot realise their full potential."
Ban Ki-moon, former UN Secretary-General

In 2020, the United Nations reported that closing the gender gap could grow global GDP by an average of 35%. Indeed, activating the potential of the world's women would go a long way towards creating a rich society – ethically and economically.

Making space for female leadership

A 14-year study of the S&P 1500 firms showed that having more female managers meant better financial performance. Meanwhile, companies with strong female leadership at the board level generate a return on equity that is a whopping 36% greater than other companies.

Research has shown that the *combination* of women and men working together provides optimal outcomes. For example, a study across 18 countries found that where countries had gender quotas in place, companies saw better market performance, stronger board vigilance and more efficient corporate governance. The third wealthiest nation, **Norway**, also ranks third in the Global Gender Gap Index, and it mandates that publicly listed companies must have a minimum of 40% of women on their boards or risk dissolution.

Other Nordic nations also prioritise female leadership – in **Iceland**, as of 2021, women hold 42% of senior or managerial posts and represent 46% of board members. **Finland**, meanwhile, has 37% representation of women in leadership roles.

In 2015, **Australia** called for the 200 largest companies on its stock exchange to improve gender representation on boards from 19% to 30% by 2018. The Workplace Gender Equality Agency required businesses with over 100 employees to report on gender equality, monitored the data and kept the public informed on Australia's progress. A key council of investors also pledged to vote against companies without female directors. By December 2019, the 30% target was achieved, with the largest 100 companies slightly exceeding it.

In 2011, the **United Kingdom** set a target of 25% female representation on the boards of its 100 largest listed companies by 2015. In 2013, it mandated disclosure of gender representation at director, senior manager and employee levels every year. In 2016, with the 25% target largely achieved, a new target of 33% representation by 2020 was introduced for the 350 largest listed businesses. The corporate governance code was revised to encourage companies to support diversity when making board appointments and planning succession. In addition, board nomination committees were made responsible for developing a diverse pipeline for senior management succession. Thanks to these efforts, female board representation has more than doubled since 2011, growing from 12.5% to 32% among the 100 largest companies and to 30% among the largest 350 companies.

Progress is being made in Africa too. **Kenya**'s 2010 constitution mandates without penalty that no corporate board should have more than two-thirds of its members from one gender. Companies are also legally required to consider gender when appointing board members. To make these targets a reality, the Federation of Kenya Employers set up the 'Female Future' programme in 2013. The programme set the goal to train approximately 300 women before 2021 and to see 60% of its graduates on at least one corporate board. Within a year, half of its initial graduates were appointed as members of boards, with about 70% reporting that they were in positions of greater responsibility.

Supporting women in STEM

Fuelling girls' interest in Science, Technology, Engineering and Mathematics (STEM) can lay the foundation for high-earning careers that enhance women's economic security, contribution and their social and political voice. Interestingly, it isn't those countries with the greatest reputation for gender equality that boast a high representation of women in STEM fields. For example, as of 2021, the largest proportion of female engineering graduates could be found in the Arab states, including **Algeria** (49%), **Tunisia** (44%) and **Oman** (43%). Compare this with France (26%), Australia (23%) and Canada (20%). It seems that overall levels of gender equality in a country have little to do with the way the country views women in science. Instead, history and culture play an important role. Consider that one of the world's oldest universities was established by a Muslim lady, Fatima Al-Fihri.

Interviews with 11,500 girls and young women across Europe by Microsoft found that girls' interest in STEM subjects declines significantly at age 15. This was found to be largely due to gender stereotyping, a lack of female role models, peer pressure and low levels of support from parents and teachers. When girls grow up, they get less credit than men for equal performance in math, and find that STEM professors are more inclined to hire 'John' than 'Jennifer', even when the applications are identical. 'Jennifer' would also earn USD 4,000 less.

But there is hope. Women comprise the majority of scientists and engineers in **Norway**, **Denmark**, **Bulgaria**, **Lithuania**, **Latvia** and **Portugal**. Meanwhile, they also outnumber men as researchers in **New Zealand**, **Tunisia**, and a handful of Asian and Latin American countries, including **Argentina**, **Georgia**, **Kazakhstan**, **Thailand** and **Venezuela**. Some of these countries actively encourage female participation in science, often in government-funded facilities.

Various nations that were members of the Soviet Union or its satellite states benefitted from an active encouragement of female participation in science, supported with government facilities. They were able to support female scientists and engineers in continuing to study and work by reducing the domestic burden expected of women. They did so by providing paid maternity leave, childcare, public laundries, public cafeterias and care facilities for the sick and elderly. From 1962 to 1964, 40% of Soviet **Russia**'s chemistry PhDs were awarded to women, contrasting starkly with 5% in the United States. Indeed, the first woman to go to space, Valentina Tereshkova, was Russian.

This visibility of female role models in STEM does make a difference. A study found that seven times more male characters than female characters are depicted as engineers, scientists and mathematicians in the United States film industry. Challenging such depictions can help alter deep-set perceptions of gender norms.

Activating women during crises

In 2017, 86% of **Rwandan** women were active in the workforce – one of the world's highest proportions, and women were earning 88 cents per dollar earned by men. The United States, comparatively, had a female labour participation rate of only 56% (and declining) and women were earning only 74 cents for every dollar earned by men.

Following the horrific genocide in Rwanda where about 800,000 people were killed, 60-70% of survivors were female, with little option but to perform the roles that men used to do to keep the economy firing. Since then, women have not looked back. Indeed, Rwanda was the world's first country to have a female majority in parliament.

The **United States** also saw a boom in women in the workforce during the Second World War, when men were at war and jobs needed to be done to keep the economy moving. Recognising the pressing need, the government initiated a nationwide campaign to persuade women to enter the labour force. It is estimated that approximately five million women joined the workforce during the period.

However, while the US is the only developed country without mandatory paid maternity leave, Rwanda provides three months of paid leave to new mothers, supporting them in returning to the workforce after having a child.

STIMULATING INNOVATION

The Bloomberg Innovation Index 2021 ranks **South Korea** in the number one spot, a position the nation has held for seven of the nine years the index has been published. It is followed by **Singapore**. Meanwhile, **Switzerland**, **Sweden**, the **United States**, the **United Kingdom** and **South Korea** lead the rankings of the Global Innovation Index 2021, while The World Intellectual Property Organisation (WIPO) has also named **Switzerland** the most innovative country in the world for more than 10 consecutive years. What makes these nations so inventive?

Funding research and development

South Korea invests an impressive 4.5% of its GDP in research and development, helping it claim its place as a world leader in innovation. In 1995, the government invested USD 1.5 billion in a 10-year initiative to develop national broadband infrastructure, alongside programmes to support the public in making the most of it. The investment has paid off, helping to produce startups (high-potential young companies) like food-delivery application Woova, valued at over USD 1 billion in 2018. **Sweden**, another innovation leader, also gave citizens a head-start in the digital age with its own national broadband network in the 1990s.

And while the rest of the EU invests an average of 2.3% of income in research and innovation, **Switzerland** puts 3.4% of its national income towards research and innovation. This generous government support is also offered with a bottom-up approach. Individuals with bright ideas are encouraged to make proposals, and the highest potential ideas are funded. By policy, funds from *Innosuisse* – the Swiss Innovation Agency – are given to universities. This encourages companies to partner with universities in product development and innovation. The collaboration supports a win-win model where universities provide subsidised research support to businesses, and those businesses ensure that universities are well connected to the rapidly evolving economy. It's no wonder Forbes deemed the country the "Silicon Valley of Robotics".

Among the EU countries, **Luxembourg** is by far the leader in research and development investment per capita, investing approximately USD 680 per inhabitant in 2021. This funding goes towards advancing knowledge via universities and other avenues, industrial production and technology, health, space technology, energy, and more.

Other nations have introduced unique methods of supporting research and development. For example, in Lisbon, **Portugal**, a biotechnology lab has been set up and made freely available to all students, entrepreneurs, researchers and citizens. The effort seeks to encourage biotechnology training, experimentation and business creation.

Creating spaces for collaboration

A mountainous nation with a population of just 8.5 million, **Switzerland** benefits from a practical and job-focused education system. This helps develop a highly skilled workforce with strong links to the economy and the capacity to produce goods and services with real market need. To encourage this market mentality, several locations nationwide connect universities and local and international businesses to network and share ideas. These sites allow scientific and economic orientations to mesh, fast-tracking innovation. The EPFL Innovation Park, set up about 25 years ago, is an example of one such site. It hosts more than 25 big businesses and about 150 high-growth startups. These companies share access to the research laboratories and other facilities of EPFL university, one of Switzerland's two federal technology institutes.

South Korea's largest company, Samsung, which accounts for about 15% of the national GDP, is also engaged in numerous university collaborations. Since the 1990s, the government has invested in developing regional innovation centres that bring together industry innovation and production facilities with universities and research laboratories. By 2010, there were 105 regional innovation centres and 18 tech parks in the country. As of 2021, South Korea boasts the leading position globally in patent registration.

Welcoming skilled immigrants

"Diversity is the engine of invention.
It generates creativity that enriches the world."
Justin Trudeau, prime minister of Canada

With over a quarter of its population represented by immigrants, **Switzerland**'s stability makes it an attractive destination for brilliant minds escaping war and persecution – Albert Einstein being one example. Thanks to an EU agreement allowing the free movement of labour, any citizen of any EU country can work in Switzerland without a visa.

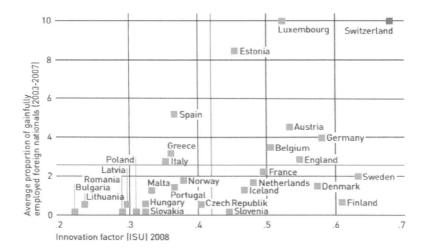

Correlation between innovation and the proportion of gainfully employed foreign nationals; Source: economiesuisse, European Scoreboard

The country's welcoming attitude towards immigrants has sped up its rate of innovation. Indeed, at the tech-oriented EPFL university, over 120 nationalities are represented and nearly half the students have roots outside the country.

Economist Jennifer Hunt confirms that welcoming skilled immigrants can add significant medium- to long-term value to an economy, with graduates seeking a Master's degree or doctorate demonstrating particular value. In the **United States**, such individuals are more likely to establish companies and register about twice as many patents compared with locals. Indeed, about 60% of US-based technology companies were founded by immigrants or the children of immigrants. Boasting the renowned Silicon Valley, many of the world's most elite universities, and a reputation for innovation, the United States attracts energetic and ambitious migrants from all over the world.

Israel, the 9-million-person country with the highest per capita density of startups and unicorns (unicorns are startups valued at over USD 1 billion), has a 'Law of Return' that invites Jews and their families from all over the world to secure citizenship in Israel. The country, which is also one of the world's most educated nations, has 140 scientists, engineers and technicians per 10,000 people (for comparison, the United States has 85).

Initiating public-private partnerships

The **United States**' position at the forefront of cutting-edge technology has helped make it one of the world's wealthiest countries in terms of GDP per capita. Historically, a great deal of innovation in the United States stemmed from partnerships between the government and the private sector – this includes radio communication, GPS, microprocessors, the Internet, and the aviation industry. The government would often be the first big buyer of experimental innovations in biomedicine, telecommunications, and electronics.

Finding a competitor

Competition between Russia and the **United States** spurred both countries to innovate more aggressively, taking greater risks to claim technological supremacy. Following 1945, the United States switched modes from adapting and improving on existing technologies to indulging a much greater appetite for risk and pouring significant resources into long-term science and technology initiatives – which paid off. Over time, this supported a culture of high tolerance for failure, public hunger for novelty, intellectual property protection, and financial backing for innovations – from venture capital funding to public stock offerings.

Digitising to minimise red tape

Technology can help bypass the bureaucracy of government service provision. It empowers citizens and companies to access government services and fulfil municipal obligations in an efficient and streamlined way. For example, the **Czech** city of Liberec has launched a Citizen Web Portal providing a single digital access point for filing forms, submitting applications, paying fees and tracking processes, eliminating the need to schedule office hours and queue at municipal departments. This enables businesses and individuals to spend more time building and innovating, beyond battling red tape.

In 2022, the **Romanian** town of Sânmartin was awarded the title of 'Most Digitalised Local Administration' for its clever efforts to encourage citizens to switch to digital avenues for accessing government services. For example, citizens who made tax payments by a certain date were offered a 10% tax rebate – provided they had paid online.

Meanwhile, many Nordic countries are becoming cashless economies. As far back as 2016, less than 20% of regional transactions were cash-based, representing a mere 1% of transaction value. Half the region's population use mobile payment apps like MobilePay, Swish and Vipps. In fact, **Sweden**'s central bank is exploring replacing cash with a digital substitute – the e-krona.

Building smart cities

Smart cities leverage technology to collect large amounts of data about the city and use it to improve the infrastructure and services available to citizens. For example, with smart bins that use technology to optimise waste management and smart mobility solutions that optimise traffic flow. Many Nordic cities, including the capitals of **Denmark, Finland, Iceland, Norway** and **Sweden**, have launched open-source data platforms. These can be freely accessed by all citizens who may use the data to research and develop smart city projects. These cities have also launched several public/private 'Living Labs' that equip entrepreneurs to build, test and execute smart city projects in real-life conditions.

FOSTERING ENTREPRENEURIAL SUCCESS

"Every single human being is creative and maximising that creativity is critical to happiness and economic growth."
Richard Florida, Director of Cities at the
Martin Prosperity Institute

Unicorn companies are private companies valued at over USD 1 billion within their first 10 years of existence. As of 2022, there were more than 1,000 unicorns worldwide. Well-known unicorn companies include Google, Facebook and Airbnb.

Outside of Silicon Valley, the Nordic countries (**Denmark, Norway, Sweden, Iceland, Finland** – and including **Estonia**) boast the world's most unicorns per capita, as of 2021. Despite accounting for just 4% of the European population, since 2005, the Nordic countries have been responsible for 9% of the world's total billion-dollar exits – more than the balance 96% of Europe.

How are the Nordic nations doing it?

Factors like free education and strong social security foster an environment where Nordic citizens can take risks without fear of failure. Among Nordic university students, 90% believe entrepreneurship is a culturally accepted avenue.

Across Europe, the Nordics also boast among the highest levels of investment in research and development. An efficient public sector that provides streamlined e-governance further supports the startup ecosystem.

The largest Nordic country, **Sweden**, also has its most robust startup ecosystem with the most unicorns and best funding prospects. As of 2021, Sweden also has the unicorns with the highest valuations – an impressive USD 10 billion on average, about double that of the nations ranked second. Its capital, Stockholm, has the largest proportion of any European capital – 20% – of its workforce attached to the technology sector. The city also boasts a high density of top-performing universities.

Meanwhile, **Denmark** treats innovation as a key element of the educational curriculum, particularly across scientific and technical departments. In fact, between 1999 and 2017, the Technical University of Denmark produced over 2,200 new businesses – a rate of over two per week! The capital, Copenhagen, has become a startup hub featuring several incubators, accelerators and co-working spaces.

Both Denmark and Sweden are not just among the top seven in the Global Innovation Index and International Corruption Index, but also the World Happiness Report – suggesting a connection between citizens' wellbeing and their capacity to innovate.

Estonia is a startup success story, with the world's highest number of startups per capita. Despite a population of just 1.3 million, the country has generated five unicorns. The secret to its success seems to be smart policy decisions that have encouraged over 50,000 founders from more than 150 countries to set up 7,000 new businesses in the country. These visionary initiatives include its e-Residency programme and Startup Visa programme which have simplified the set-up process and inspired entrepreneurs to leverage Estonia as a platform to scale across the EU. Estonian legislation is startup-friendly and the government actively supports the startup community. As we saw before, the education system also fosters entrepreneurship, with students given real-world experience through work placements, which form a major part of both vocational and academic education. The country's rigorous efforts have paid off, and the nation has made a name in cybersecurity and fintech.

The **United States** is the world leader when it comes to unicorn volume, accounting for just over half of the world's unicorns as of 2023. One in five of the nation's unicorns are internet and software companies, and the country holds the top spot in several high-value sectors such as fintech. With a large proportion of entrepreneurially-minded migrants, access to risk capital from investors, and some of the world's most prestigious educational establishments, the nation has the right ingredients to foster startup success.

Other nations are also making bold efforts to boost entrepreneurship. The youth of Venice, **Italy**, can participate in free idea incubators at city libraries. Here, they engage in practical laboratories where they test prototypes, determine how best to market products and evaluate economic sustainability based on hypothetical sales projections. The goal is to develop entrepreneurially-minded youth who have the skills to succeed as innovators.

Meanwhile, over in the **German** state of North Rhine-Westphalia, students are informed about the process of creating a startup, provided with case studies of young founders, and empowered with a network of mentors and connections to answer their questions.

10

Inclusivity
Universal kindness and respect

*"We have the ability to achieve – if we master
the necessary goodwill – a common global society
blessed with a shared culture of peace."*
Mahnaz Afkhami, Iranian-American human rights activist

In Utopia, every person would feel profoundly valued, whatever their race, religion, skin colour, nationality, gender, sexuality, socioeconomic status, or whether or not they have a disability. Kindness would be extended to animals too and compassion would go beyond national borders.

Some countries have made efforts to make such a world a reality. Let's consider what we can learn from them in designing a utopia for all.

SUPPORTING HARMONY IN DIVERSITY

Actively preserving harmony

Since securing independence in 1965, **Singapore** has carefully nurtured a multi-religious national identity that celebrates social harmony. Although the country's population comprises Chinese, Malays and Indians, the English language is prioritised as a link language to avoid the emphasis on any one ethnic group over another. In addition, government-provided flats (where over 80% of Singaporeans live) are required by law to reflect the nation's ethnic diversity when providing residency. This prevents the formation of racial or ethnic ghettos.

It's illegal to fuel hatred or ill will between faith communities, with codes of conduct around religious harmony. There is a Presidential Council of Minority Rights to protect minorities, and the government encourages communication with and between religious groups.

"Our ability to reach unity in diversity
will be the beauty and the test of our civilisation."
Mahatma Gandhi, Indian lawyer

Illustrating the level of priority it gives the topic, the country also has a Presidential Council for Religious Harmony and a Maintenance of Religious Harmony Act. Among other items, the Act encourages individuals who have offended another religious group to make amends via an apology and engage in activities such as inter-religious events to better understand the affected community. While this is optional, refusing to do so is factored in when considering whether a case would be referred for criminal prosecution. The Act also covers immediate issuance of a restraining order on those who circulate offensive online content.

Another measure of the Act is to require that any affiliations with foreign organisations or people holding positions of power and/or foreign donations of over USD 10,000 to a religious group must be declared. These can be restricted if deemed to undermine religious harmony.

Acknowledging past wrongs

While apologies from governments can seem like an inadequate response to massive injustices in a nation's past, they are an important first step to begin a process of healing. They acknowledge the suffering caused, raise historical consciousness and challenge the country to do better going forward. A complete national apology accounts fully for what occurred and why it happened, demonstrates empathy for what the victims experienced and its long-term impacts, accepts responsibility and seeks to make amends.

"The consequences of history are not dissolved by time. They actually remain present in the lives and communities and contexts of many people." Charlotte Macdonald, New Zealand historian

In 2019, **New Zealand** prime minister Jacinda Ardern made a formal apology on behalf of the New Zealand government for the Dawn Raids of the 1970s where police discriminatorily enforced immigration laws, performing raids on the homes of Pacific communities. The apology acknowledged that mere words were not sufficient and promised to support the development of a historical account of the Dawn Raids for educational purposes alongside approximately USD 1.97 million in educational and short-term training scholarships and fellowships for Pacific communities. During the apology ceremony, a fine mat was placed over the prime minister as a Samoan gesture to represent remorse in seeking forgiveness. New Zealand has issued other apologies previously, including an apology to Chinese New Zealanders for historic discrimination and taxation, along with a heritage fund of about USD 3 million for the community.

Effective apologies can have a powerful impact on recipients. Aunty Lorain Peeters was one of the kidnapped aboriginal children of Australia who was taken from her family to be raised in a white home. She described the day in 2008 when the **Australian** prime minister Kevin Rudd apologised as "a day I will never, ever forget in my life, because we were being acknowledged as a group of people".

Setting an example of compassion

Following an attack by a white supremacist on the Muslim community of **New Zealand**, prime minister Jacinda Ardern demonstrated her solidarity with the minority community. She visited the mosques in hijab, hugged and consoled community members, spoke out against racism and discrimination, and refused to use the attacker's name. Ardern also followed through with practical measures such as strict gun legislation. Her empathy in preaching unity set an example for the rest of the country, which followed her lead with an overwhelming flood of support and compassion for New Zealand's Muslim community.

In **Czechia**, the city of Pilsen is demonstrating compassion in healthcare, with paramedics provided with communication cards in multiple languages. The cards contain basic queries (such as 'Are you in pain?') that paramedics need to find out in the event of an emergency. These can support them in serving people who speak languages which differ from their own, as well as non-verbal individuals.

The **Belgian** city of Ghent, meanwhile, is using a unique method to introduce the concept of inclusivity at a young age – by distributing to schools a free collection of 'skin colour' coloured pencils featuring every shade of skin colour. The pencils aim to support teachers in holding conversations about diversity and discrimination, tackling racism at a young age.

Leveraging immigration for national success

> *"The best economies in the world have grown on the back*
> *of an environment that is tolerant and accepting."*
> *Patrice Motsepe, African founder and billionaire*

Based on a 2019 Gallup poll of over 140,000 people across 145 countries and regions, **Canada** emerged as the nation most welcoming towards migrants. It was followed by **Iceland**, **New Zealand** and **Australia**. The poll asked people their thoughts about migrants living in their country, being their neighbours and marrying into their families.

Countries like Canada view immigration as a valuable way to combat the effects of an ageing population and a low birth rate. This is a real problem in a country where the number of workers to retirees has dropped from six in 1980 to four in 2015. By 2030, it will be down to just three. Thanks to immigrants, employers have access to a growing labour force of qualified employees who can fill available posts. This workforce further supports the economy by paying taxes that cover healthcare and other supports for the retired. Having a wider pool of workers helps reduce the income tax that any one worker has to pay. Immigrants also spend on goods and services like homes and transportation. Canada even has an Express Entry programme inviting skilled workers to immigrate.

While myths about immigrants continue to persist, many have proven untrue. For example, data from the United States and the United Kingdom demonstrate that immigrants are, in fact, less likely to end up in prison than the local population.

VALUING LGBT+ COMMUNITIES

Individuals who identify among sexual and gender minorities, such as lesbian, gay, bisexual or transgender (LGBT), often experience discrimination – sometimes from their own families, teachers, employers, religious community, and society in general. A lack of acceptance of sexual and gender minorities is connected with violence, bullying, physical and mental health issues, discrimination in employment and a lack of representation in political leadership. It can also reduce workplace productivity and corporate profits. In fact, those countries that provide more rights to individuals who identify as lesbian, gay and bisexual benefit from significantly greater GDP per capita. Even a single extra point on the legal rights scale corresponds with a boost in real GDP per capita of over USD 2,000.

Around the world, many factors influence the acceptance of LGBT+ people. There is a strong correlation between the wealth of an economy and its levels of LGBT+ acceptance. In addition, younger members of society are far more likely to be accepting. For example, while 79% of 18-to-29-year-olds in South Korea, approved of homosexuality in 2019, this drops to 51% among 30-to-49-year-olds, and still further to 23% among those over 50. Religiosity also tends to reduce acceptance. And in the few countries where men and women show significantly different levels of acceptance, women are more likely to approve of homosexuality.

As of 2020, the Global Acceptance Index recognises **Iceland**, the **Netherlands**, **Norway**, **Sweden** and **Canada** as the most accepting countries. These nations actively promote the acceptance of LGBT+ individuals with legislation prohibiting discrimination and supporting equal marriage, partnership and adoption.

Legislating for inclusion

France made homosexuality legal as far back as 1791, and 125 countries have followed suit. In 2001, the **Netherlands** was the first country to legalise gay marriage. Since then, approximately 30 countries have come to recognise same-sex marriages. They include **Belgium**, **Luxembourg**, **Spain** and **Brazil**.

In the **United Kingdom**, where Queen Elizabeth II gave royal assent to legalising same-sex marriage in England and Wales, primary school children are taught about different types of families. This helps to normalise families featuring two mothers or two fathers. During Angela Merkel's time as chancellor, besides permitting gay marriage and adoption, **Germany** also banned gay conversion therapy on children.

Today, more than 25 nations worldwide permit same-sex couples to adopt children, once again led by the **Netherlands**. These countries include **Denmark**, **France**, **Ireland**, **South Africa** and **Israel**, with more than half situated in Europe.

In 1977, the **Canadian** state of Quebec became the first jurisdiction to outlaw discrimination against sexual minorities. The **Netherlands** also protects its LGBT+ community with laws against hate speech about whom individuals love, their gender identity and expression. And in **Iceland** too, it is illegal to discriminate based on perceived or actual gender identity.

Legalisation accelerates social change – within four years of legalising gay marriage, the **United States** saw a boost in the level of acceptance of LGBT+ persons that was nearly equivalent to that in the 15 years before legalisation.

Recognising non-binary rights

Since as far back as 1543, **Finland** has had in its language the personal pronoun hän. This third-person singular pronoun is gender-neutral, representing both 'she' and 'he'.

In 2013, **Germany** became the first in the European Union to add a third gender to birth certificates to accommodate babies born without clear gender-determining biological features.

But it is **Canada** that has one of the world's most progressive transgender laws, allowing citizens to change their gender on legal documentation without undergoing gender reassignment surgery. The country also recognises a third gender option. In the **United Kingdom**, the title 'Mx' is accepted as a non-binary alternative to 'Ms' and 'Mr' in government and business institutions. And the National Health Service makes treatment for gender dysphoria freely available to all citizens.

Apart from allowing individuals to choose their legal gender recognition, in **Argentina**, sex-change surgery is deemed a right covered by public and private insurance.

Appointing LGBT+ leaders

While **Iceland** had the first openly gay head of state in the world (prime minister Jóhanna Sigurðardóttir) in 2009, **New Zealand**'s 2020 parliament has perhaps the largest proportion of LGBT+ lawmakers. Here, 11% of parliamentarians identify as LGBT+, including the deputy prime minister.

Before New Zealand, it was the **United Kingdom** that elected a record 7% of LGBT+ candidates to parliament in 2017. Meanwhile, as of 2020, 5% of **Israeli** lawmakers are openly gay.

Celebrating the LGBT+ community

Several countries celebrate and recognise the LGBT+ community by hosting Pride events. Toronto Pride, in **Canada**, is one of the world's largest Pride events and attracts nearly 1.5 million individuals every year. Canadian prime minister Justin Trudeau has enthusiastically participated in gay pride parades.

In 2019, the country celebrated the 50th anniversary of its decriminalisation of homosexuality by introducing a new $1 coin (loonie). In doing so, it became the first country to recognise the LGBT+ community on its currency.

The **Netherlands** honoured the community in 1987 by unveiling the *"Homomonument"*, a monument to memorialise gays and lesbians persecuted during World War Two.

And the **United States** made history in 2015 when it lit up the White House in rainbow colours to recognise its Supreme Court ruling allowing same-sex couples to marry.

ENSURING DISABILITY INCLUSIVITY

Upholding disability rights

In 2015, **Uganda** had 47 individuals with disabilities in politics. The country's multiple civil wars have left a higher proportion of people facing disability but, as a result, the country is now known for having some of the world's most progressive disability rights. These include five reserved seats in parliament for people with disabilities, as well as quotas at district, village, parish and sub-county levels for disability representation. Beyond the quotas, parliamentarians with disabilities have also been elected through the standard process. Other African countries have sent delegations to learn about the Ugandan model in efforts to replicate it back home.

The Ugandan education system includes a national training programme for educators of those with disabilities and a combination of integrated and disability-specific schools. Disability is regularly discussed in mass media, across newspapers, radio talk shows and television programmes. Meanwhile, Uganda's National Council for Disability is just one of the offices that oversee disability rights and contribute to policy decisions.

All of these efforts are the outcome of disability activists and advocates who have been speaking up for disability rights since the 1970s. Their work is not over yet, however, as while the laws are progressive, implementation is often poor.

Croatia has an Ombudswoman for Persons with Disabilities. This office manages complaints about discrimination against persons with disabilities across employment, education, housing, social protection and healthcare, goods and services, as well as other areas, and covers both the public and private sectors. It also independently monitors the country's implementation of the UN Convention on the rights of persons with disabilities.

Implementing universal design

Norway is among the few countries that legally deem a lack of accessibility as a form of discrimination. Initiatives such as 'Norway Universally Designed by 2025' strive to achieve a lived environment that is usable by as many people as possible – whether they have disabilities, are elderly or have small children in pushchairs. This can mean replacing steps with slopes and elevators, making the heights of counters or desks adjustable, automating the opening and closing of doors, ensuring the availability of touchable safety markers and braille lettering, providing both audio and visual support, and designing simply and intuitively. The universal design of buildings, transport, outdoor spaces and technology reduces exclusion from education and working life and improves economic standards of living for those with disabilities. Norway's public administration sector has adopted universal design, requiring that all new buildings and facilities be universally designed. In addition, existing buildings, facilities and outdoor spaces will be upgraded over time, taking advantage of planned maintenance and repair efforts.

The capital of the **Netherlands**, Amsterdam, is using big data and artificial intelligence to identify areas of the city with poor accessibility and assist citizens with disabilities in navigating the city. Online users can train the Project Sidewalk machine learning algorithm by using the software to take a virtual walk around the city and mark accessibility issues such as missing sidewalks, broken curb ramps, a lack of signage, sidewalk obstacles, surface issues, etc. With time, the software will learn to flag issues on its own and the information will assist policymakers in correcting problems.

The **French** capital Paris also introduced efforts to make the city more accessible ahead of hosting the 2024 Olympic and Paralympic Games. The city offered up to around USD 10,000 to retailers who wish to make their shops more accessible to people with disabilities, with features such as accessible fitting rooms, restrooms and checkout facilities, non-slip floor coverings, floor markings and Braille signage.

In the **German** capital of Berlin, public toilets are designed to accommodate individuals with disabilities. The toilets are fully automated and can also be located via an app.

The **Croatian** capital of Zagreb has introduced a tourist map for wheelchair users – accessible in both print and digital formats. The 'Blue Line map' highlights wheelchair-accessible routes and suggested directions for exploring 12 of the city's landmarks. Similarly, in the

Greek capital of Athens, eight accessible routes have been mapped a dedicated website to support people with motor and visual impairments in exploring the city. The routes highlight both ancient and modern landmarks and are accompanied by general accessibility information as well as details on public transport and restroom accessibility.

Athens also supports the deaf and hard of hearing within its municipal clinics. A tablet at the location lets users access the services of a professional Greek sign language interpreter. The remote interpretation service helps patients converse with doctors and nurses and enable a smooth healthcare experience.

Accessible public transport can dramatically transform the level of freedom that individuals with disabilities enjoy. The **Spanish** city of Barcelona understands this. It supports visually impaired residents in navigating public transport with tactile routes, loudspeakers at stations and on trains, radio beacon guidance, Braille and high-relief on the buttons on elevators, scannable signage, vending machines with a voice navigation system, Braille signs in buses and audio notices about the next stop. The latest addition is Braille sticker signage with stop information on the handrails at metro stations and bus stops.

Meanwhile, **Latvia** has had dedicated libraries for the sight-impaired since 1962. Today, the libraries provide audiobooks, Braille books, tactile books, large print books and mixed media books. And the collection of accessible literature is constantly growing thanks to a Braille production department and sound recording studio that regularly churn out new material.

Over in the **Spanish** city of Valencia, efforts have been made to help individuals on the autism spectrum safely cross the street. Pictograms painted onto the pedestrian crossing depict the steps involved – stop, look, check the traffic light, cross at the walk signal. These signs help individuals with autism logically sequence the actions needed to safely cross the street.

Malta, meanwhile, boasts several institutions that have achieved autism-friendly accreditation, including the airport, national aquarium, museums and entertainment venues. The McDonald's at the Malta International Airport became the country's first autism-friendly restaurant by introducing a room with unique features, including dimmer lighting, low noise levels, noise-cancelling headphones and sensory playthings. Additionally, every Monday and Thursday from 3:00 pm to 4:30 pm, the entire restaurant maintains dim lighting and low noise levels. Employees have been trained to become 'Autism Ambassadors' equipped to support the needs of customers with autism.

In **Denmark**, technology plays a key part in improving the quality of life of those with disabilities. For example, a teenage boy suffering from a lung condition that prevents him from physically attending school can remotely control a 5G robot in the classroom. The desktop robot can turn to provide a view of all sides of the classroom and enables the student to chat with peers through audio and video. This provides a sense of independence in navigating the school environment.

Providing meaningful employment

The World Economic Forum has reported that hiring individuals with disabilities benefits businesses – they can enjoy reduced turnover, greater profitability, and stronger reputations among customers. It also boosts the quality of life of those with disabilities, giving them economic opportunities and a greater sense of purpose.

A programme in **Norway** subsidises about 2,000 companies that recruit about 1,700 people with disabilities a year. It also covers the cost of assistive equipment, and offers support and training to employees with disabilities, along with wage subsidies if they require extended medical leave. Assistive aid centres are present in every county to support anyone injured or impaired in getting and retaining jobs. Employers are also trained to support individuals with disabilities in delivering their best. As of 2019, 44% of those with disabilities between the ages of 15 and 66 were employed. This is a start, though those without disabilities are still 30% more likely to have a job.

In the **Danish** Municipality of Aarhus, youth with autism are taught subjects which are increasingly in demand, including green technology and sustainability, to support them in securing employment. The city has worked with the National Association for Autism to ensure that the school effectively meets its students' needs.

PROTECTING ANIMAL WELFARE

Opting for a cruelty-free diet

As of 2020, **India** and **Tanzania** take the top spots for animal welfare, according to the Voiceless Animal Cruelty Index. While these countries do not necessarily have robust legislation to protect animals, far less animal slaughter occurs. This is because these countries slaughter only two animals per person per year, a fifth of the world average of more than 10. Over 80% of Indian adults restrict their meat consumption, and nearly 40% identify as vegetarian. Meanwhile, Tanzania has an extensive, rather than intensive, farming system which allows animals to freely graze outdoors and move around at will.

Certain other countries are seeing a decline in meat consumption. In **Germany**, for example, over 40% of people are cutting back on meat, intentionally opting for a vegan, vegetarian, pescatarian or 'flexitarian' diet. As of 2020, Germans who eat meat without restrictions are a minority, and 10% of the population is vegetarian. As The Guardian put it, 'the wurst is over'.

Switzerland, **Denmark** and **Norway** are among the countries that require animals to be stunned before slaughter. **Sweden** also requires that farmed animals be sedated, protecting them from pain and fear. Sow stalls and farrowing crates, which are highly confining, are banned – instead, sows must be able to easily move and turn. Battery cages for chickens are also illegal, and in the summer, dairy animals must be allowed to graze outdoors. In addition, the lighting, temperature, humidity, air circulation, ventilation and other environmental conditions (e.g. drinkers, feeding, litter, noise) within farms are also specified to improve the animals' comfort.

Legislating to ensure protection

Austria is among the countries affording the most rights to animals. Its Animal Welfare Act equates the importance of animal life to that of human life. It prohibits causing animal suffering, unjustified pain, exposure to heavy fear, and most forms of injury. This includes farm animals, with rules specifically in place for their protection, such as a prohibition on farmers caging their chickens. Wild animals cannot be used in circuses, fur farming is banned and great apes cannot be used in experiments. Pet owners are prohibited from cropping their dogs' ears or tails, and puppies and kittens cannot be made to swelter in pet shop windows.

In the **United Kingdom**, there are significant penalties for cruelty and negligence towards animals, including fines amounting to approximately USD 24,000, jail time of up to 51 weeks and a lifetime ban from pet ownership. Meanwhile, in **Hong Kong**, those who violate animal cruelty laws can be fined about USD 26,000 and imprisoned for three years.

In a move supported by the majority of residents, Amsterdam in the **Netherlands** banned fireworks on New Year's Eve. This not only minimises human injury and reduces waste, but gives local animals –

many of whom experience acute distress at this time of year – a comfortable New Year's Eve.

Encouraging adoption

In the **United States**, the animal welfare organisation ASPCA goes above and beyond to help stray dogs and cats find caring homes. The animals are even transported across state lines to places with fewer available animals and greater demand for pets. This relocation practice has saved over 200,000 animals from being euthanised by giving them new homes.

In May 2022, the **Greek** municipality of Maroussi conducted a festival to introduce potential pet owners to stray animals so they could fall in love. The festival boasted animal mascots, face painting, raffles, music and an educational show – all to encourage individuals to give stray animals a loving home.

Businesses are also making an effort to support animal adoption. At **Poland**'s Bunny Café, customers can enjoy a cup of coffee, play with the resident rescue rabbits and consider adopting a fluffy new family member. The Kitty Café in the **United Kingdom** follows a similar format, rehoming dozens of rescue cats. Clear regulations for interacting with the animals help to ensure their wellbeing.

Over in the **Portuguese** city of Famalicão, stray cats are sterilised to prevent unchecked breeding. Since each female cat can produce 18 kittens a year, sterilisation helps reduce the population of homeless and unfed cats. The sterilised cats are then provided with sheltered spaces where community members bring them food and help with shelter maintenance and upkeep.

Meanwhile, in the capital, Lisbon, free veterinary services are provided to socially disadvantaged pet owners, and social workers are accompanied by vets. Services include deworming, vaccination, veterinary treatments and electronic identification. Food, hygiene products and temporary shelter are also made available to furry friends.

Protecting land areas

Planet Earth is home to about 10 million animal species. Preserving natural habitats helps ensure those species have a safe space to thrive. Some countries take this responsibility seriously. For example, over 55% of **Venezuela**'s land mass is protected by law. The country has over 40 national parks, with every state having at least one park. These protected lands are home to about 14% of the world's bird species, 10% of the earth's plant species, and about 7% of the world's mammals, including giant anteaters, cougars and giant otters.

SHARING WITHIN AND BEYOND BORDERS

Fostering generous citizens

> *"Unless someone like you cares a whole awful lot,*
> *nothing is going to get better. It's not."*
> *Dr Seuss, American children's author*

The Charities Aid Foundation World Giving Index, based on Gallup data, identified **Indonesia** as the world's most generous nation in 2021. More than eight in ten Indonesians donated money in the previous year and the nation's volunteering rate is more than three times the global average. Despite the COVID-19 pandemic, Indonesians continued to practice 'Zakat', a traditional form of Islamic charitable giving, and overcame social distancing regulations through online fundraising and giving platforms. In fact, online donations grew by 72% during the COVID-19 pandemic. Influencers used their social media platforms to aid relief efforts, with one Instagram influencer raising nearly USD 500,000 within a week.

New Zealand also performs well as the only country, over the 10 years of 2009 to 2019, to feature in the top 10 on all three giving measures on the World Giving Index: helping a stranger, donating money and volunteering time. Alongside Australia, its scores have also remained highly consistent over the period.

Governments have the power to accelerate giving behaviour. The Charities Aid Foundation has reported that, by optimising factors such as how charities are legislated, whether they can publicly raise funds, and the administrative ease of giving, governments can boost citizens' motivations to give.

Some governments have even adopted creative ways of encouraging charitable behaviour. For example, as part of **Poland**'s largest charity event, the mayors of various cities put their time and talents up for auction. The Mayor of Wroclaw offered a meal cooked and delivered by himself (attracting bids of around USD 700), as well as an opportunity to play tennis with him (going for about USD 900 at the last count). Other mayors offered the chance to share a cup of coffee and a chat, or score an autographed scooter or item of clothing.

Embracing cultural giving practices

Religious and cultural giving practices have a major role to play. **Indonesia**'s top spot is connected with the Islamic practice of charitable giving called 'Zakat'. The government supports the national Zakat collection body in giving grants to the United Nations for Sustainable Development Goal (SDG) related projects such as installing micro hydropower plants for remote Indonesian communities.

In **Sri Lanka**, which had the highest rate of volunteering in the world over the 10 years from 2009 to 2019, Theravada Buddhism is reputed to influence citizen generosity. Here, regular almsgivings for those leading monastic lives are common. Similarly, in **Myanmar**, the country where people are most likely to have donated money to charity, nearly 90% of the population follows Theravada Buddhism.

As of 2021, six of the ten countries where people were most likely to help a stranger were located in Africa. This is likely to be because of the philosophy of 'Ubuntu' practised by people across nearly all of Africa – this concept prizes collective humanity and mutual caring. In **Kenya**, the growing middle class gives away an impressive 22% of its monthly income. This generosity is widely credited to the culture of 'Harambee' which means 'all pull together' in Kenya's national language of Kiswahili.

Creating communal giving spaces

Across **Iran**, everyday walls have been reimagined into sites of generosity, decked out with bright paint, a simple row of hooks, and the words "Wall of Kindness: Take what you need, leave what you don't". Here, people will leave clothes they no longer need for those who would value them. Coats, jackets, jeans and more hang off the walls, sometimes accompanied by a shelf of shoes below. In a country where the capital alone has over 15,000 homeless people, Iranians have taken matters into their own hands to help. Some shops have even put out refrigerators, inviting the community to leave any extra food they may have for the homeless to take.

A 'wall of kindness' encourages citizens to share with those in need; Source: Jeremy Segrott, Flickr

Offering tax incentives

Tax incentives (like tax deductions or tax credits) boost charitable giving. In fact, where they exist, people were 12% more likely to have made a donation in the past month. The effect is even greater in low-income countries. More generous incentives lead to more donations, especially when a wide range of causes are incentivised, incentives can be claimed easily and there's little complexity in the process. Countries are also generally better off choosing between tax deductions and tax credits rather than attempting to offer both. In countries where most charitable organisations can participate in tax incentive programmes and the process for doing so is uncomplicated, the portion of the population that donates is nearly twice as high! **Canada**, **Ireland**, **Italy** and **Singapore** all have effective tax incentive programmes.

Interestingly, there is also evidence that increasing income tax rates boosts individual donations by reducing the marginal cost of giving.

Contributing to a better world

Fewer than 10 countries have met the United Nations target of contributing 0.7% of Gross National Income towards foreign aid. But **Sweden** has been doing so since 1975. And since 2008, it has set and maintained its own standard, making a long-term commitment to spending about 1% of its GNI on overseas development assistance. As of 2020, Sweden is the biggest contributor in proportional terms, contributing 1.14% of its GNI towards foreign aid. As the first country to introduce a 'feminist foreign policy', gender equality and women's empowerment are key areas of contribution for Sweden. Sweden is also the highest per-capita contributor to the Global Environment Facility and the Green Climate Fund. Other generous nations that have met or exceeded the UN target include Norway, Luxembourg, Denmark, Germany and the United Kingdom.

WHAT'S NEXT?

"I like to envision the whole world as a jigsaw puzzle ... If you look at the whole picture, it is overwhelming and terrifying, but if you work on your little part of the jigsaw and know that people all over the world are working on their little bits, that's what will give you hope."

Jane Goodall, English primatologist and anthropologist

Now that you have an idea of what makes for a utopian world, what should you do? The good news is that you don't have to sit around and wait for your country to implement these ideas. You can take action to help make them a reality in your own community.

Here are some ideas on how to start making change today:

- Send a copy of this book to a local politician, along with a letter describing three changes you are passionate about seeing within your community
- Consider initiating your own second-hand store, digital literacy caravan or other utopian project
- Discuss these ideas with friends and family, in person and on social media
- Make smart voting decisions that will support a utopian world

You have an important role to play in building our ideal future, so don't hesitate to take action.

READ THIS NEXT: 'CHANGEMAKER'

Over 50 tried-and-tested ways to change the world

For centuries, passionate people have made a difference by caring about the planet and its people. Like them, you too can change the world. Discover 50 unique strategies that more than 70 changemakers from over 20 countries have used to make an impact.

Find out:

- How two sisters went on hunger strike to clean up their island
- How a 6-year-old helped save hundreds of dogs
- How a teenager with a 3D printer is changing lives
- Why a 21-year-old donated his kidney to a math teacher
- How a rap video helped factory workers in India
- Why a billionaire is giving away 99% of their wealth
- How a graffiti artist in Afghanistan empowered women
- How a person who couldn't see envisioned a movement
- And discover dozens of other stories of changemakers across the world

Instead of feeling overwhelmed by the world's troubles, you can now learn the diverse techniques of ordinary people who have made impressive change and apply your time and talents to transforming the world. *Changemaker* will give you the motivation and direction to make it happen.

Visit www.amazon.com/dp/B0CP2YCP68 or use your phone and scan the code to learn more.

BIBLIOGRAPHY

Access links to every book, journal and article referenced in *The Utopia Playbook* by scanning this code or visiting www.cheatsheets.life/index.php/utopia.

SPREAD THE WORD

If you would like to help spread the message of *The Utopia Playbook*, here are a few more things you can do:

Gift copies to family and friends

 We need as many as possible working towards making utopia a reality. If you enjoyed *The Utopia Playbook* and would like to gift someone else a copy, visit www.amazon.com/dp/B0BT8HGVQV or scan this code.

Share your rating or review

 Ratings and reviews can encourage others to read the book and act on utopian ideas. Scan this code or visit www.amazon.com/dp/B0BT8HGVQV to place your rating or review.

ABOUT THE AUTHOR

Ayesha S. Ratnayake (MBA, Chartered Marketer) has over 10 years of experience in marketing and management.

Ayesha is a Sri Lankan based in Colombo, and was born in Suva, Fiji. She has served as CEO, Director and Shareholder of a technology firm where she led the development of an enterprise software product. She has also served as Co-founder and Director of a marketing communications agency. She is a startup mentor, mental health advocate, and the author of *Cheat Sheets for Life* and the *Love Your Life Workbook*. She can be contacted at hi@cheatsheets.life.

Learn more about
Cheat Sheets for Life

www.amazon.com/
dp/B08TYQ4HH8

Learn more about the
Love Your Life Workbook

www.amazon.com/
dp/B09Y5VVN48

COUNTRY INDEX

"How wonderful it is that nobody needs to wait a single moment before starting to improve the world."
Anne Frank, Jewish Holocaust victim

Made in the USA
Columbia, SC
05 September 2024

f30299ba-442b-4b2b-824c-5fef23d5919fR01